S0-BZV-707

ALONG THE CORKLINE

✳

12/17/2011

*To Bud & Kathy,
my very special
friends,*

Gary Kester

Veribus in the 1930's when the galley was below deck

ALONG THE CORKLINE

BY GARY KEISTER

Copyright © 2011 by Gary Keister

All rights reserved.
ISBN 978-0-615-50999-0

Printed by Gorham Printing, Centralia, Washington

To my favorite crew....
Megan, Emily, Lily
Jake, Delaney, Travis,
Lucy, Gracie, Miles,
Wes, Zane, Vlade,
Stella & Viviana
With love

CONTENTS

ACKNOWLEDGMENTS

DURING THE TIME that I have been writing this book it has been enjoyable to reminisce over the joys of my childhood and youth. It has also brought to mind so many of the men that I had worked with who were so much a part of my growing up years.

First, I must appreciate my mother Helen for her love and for her faith in allowing me at the age of 8 to go to sea with my grandfather as his cabin boy.

A very special thank you to my gifted wife Susan for her encouragement and assistance in editing and testing the recipes. Also my appreciation to Julie Knott and Tina Madsen for their advice and assistance.

To my many mentors: Francis Barcott, Les Senff, Tony Francin, Tony "Pule" Barcot, George "Jure" Franulovich, Rudolph Franulovich, Charlie Greenwood, Leon Pretti, Dominic Svornich, and Tony Martinez. Each of these men, in his own special way, instructed me in a special skill including learning how to mend web, splice lines, construct a purse seine that fished properly, set a net, read tides and currents, and recognize when a storm was brewing. Most of all I remember their patience and love of the sea.

And to the state of Alaska, of which there is no equal for having blessed me with its overwhelming beauty, glorious heritage, and the preeminent seafood of the world.

I thank the many hard working fishermen, tender men and cannery workers, many of whom are now deceased, for their recipes, yarns and patience with me as a young kid.

I remember and appreciate Dr. John Armenia, my cook on the Whitworth and Mike Seiler both friends of over forty years who are now deceased and to Fred Knapp my oldest boyhood chum all of whom provided many of the photographs included in this work.

ix

DEDICATION

To my grandfather, John Tasovac who died in 1957. He imparted to me the mysteries of the wily salmon. He was a skipper, fisherman, devoted husband, loving father, a friend to many and the best grandfather a boy could have. Grandpa John had the patience of Job, and with that splendid trait trained dozens of young men in Anacortes to become the best seamen and skippers in the North Pacific.

Fisher People

The villagers seldom
smiled or laughed.

The fishermen busied themselves
with their needles and their nets.

Children played without
ball or bat.

Old men didn't talk of
politics or religion.

Are we more contented?
Their salmon return every spring.

Metlakatla, Alaska 1962

CHAPTER ONE

The Early Years

WHEN I WAS 8 YEARS OLD in the summer of 1948, I went fishing with my grandfather John D. Tasovac. This was not just your ordinary weekend trip to a local lake for the opening of trout season. I went to sea as my grandfather's cabin boy on his salmon purse seiner, the F/V Veribus. We sailed out of our homeport in Anacortes, Washington, a picturesque fishing village on the north side of Fidalgo Island.

Anacortes is situated about 72 miles northwest of Seattle and adjoins the mainland by a bridge, which crosses the Swinomish Slough. Anacortes is known for being the gateway to the famous San Juan Islands, an archipelago of more than 170 islands, in upper Puget Sound. The islands are near the Canadian border, south of the Strait of Georgia and east of Juan de Fuca Strait. The islands, part of a submerged mountain chain, were explored and named by the Spanish Francisco Eliza expedition between 1790 and 1792.

The Veribus was a purse seiner that deployed a type of net when secured around the bottom trapped the fish. She was built in 1917 in Docton, Washington. The Veribus was long and narrow with an ivory-white hull and cabin and a sleek black trim. The smokestack had a big black "V" painted on it. She was narrow, 13' and cut through the water subtly, producing a moderate wake.

There were eight bunks for the crew in the fo'c's'le. The crew built a bunk for me adjacent to the engine over a workbench where supplies were stored. During the workday it swung up and attached to the bulkhead. The captain's cabin adjoined the wheelhouse on the main deck immediately in front of the

1

galley. The galley was always spotless with a specific location for every kitchen utensil. It was designed so everything could be batted down in the case of bad weather. The Veribus was 51 feet in length and had a draft of 6.6 feet. I thought she was the finest looking boat in the fleet.

My grandfather would start early each spring preparing the Veribus for the season. After school, I would run down to the Shell dock where the Veribus was moored. I scraped rust, painted decks or completed any number of other chores.

I remember we would move the boat each spring from our moorage around to the dry dock on the Guemes Channel. Grandpa would have her bottom surveyed and then have "Liberty" Gus, his good friend do any required caulking. Gus Lundberg was the owner and skipper of the Liberty, another Anacortes purse seiner. It was a kick to listen to them talk, Grandpa with his thick Croatian accent and Gus with his heavy Norwegian twang. I am not sure either of them knew what the other was saying half the time. I still have my grandfather's ancient caulking hammer that Gus used. After Gus was done with the caulking the shipyard crew would do the annual copper painting of the bottom and then paint the hull a rich, vanilla white.

There is no longer a Shell dock. That area is is now known as the Cap Sante Boat Haven which has over 950 slips. In the 1940s there may have been a dozen fishing boats and no more than three or four pleasure boats moored at the Shell dock. I knew the docks well, as I lived just a few blocks away on 8th Street. The docks were my play yard.

There was also a small crab processing plant on the dock operated by the Wiggins family. It gave the crab fishermen a local market for their catch.

In late May we started preparing the net for the season. The first step was tarring the new web. In those days the webbing was made of cotton and it had to be preserved in order to last a season or two. (The webbing now is made from synthetic materials and doesn't need to be treated.) The tarring process was messy and not fun. One strip of web was 220 meshes in depth and usually about 100 fathoms in length. It was placed in a large tank similar to a large old-fashioned washing machine which held the heavy liquid black tar. The web was pulled through a wringer to remove the excess liquid then taken to a grass field and spread out to dry. It would take three to four days before it was ready to be used to make the net. When I returned home from a day of this work I was literally a tar baby from head to toe.

While we did the tarring, my grandmother, Palma Tasovac prepared our lunch. She was a distinguished cook and I remember many of her delicious meals including chicken rizot, pasta with oxtails and her delicious asparagus omelet. She also prepared a terrific apple cake which was moist and delicious.

When I was in high school and playing sports Grandma often prepared my game-day meal. It was always a treat. She was also known for her exceptional dandelion wine which she shared with family and close friends.

A net commonly used in Puget Sound was about 300 fathoms in length and 7½ strips in depth. It was much deeper than the gear used in Alaska due to the exceptional depth of the water in Puget Sound. The net itself was made up of the web, cork line, and lead line. The strip of web nearest the cork line to which it was sewn was much heavier than the other strips. The strip nearest the lead line had a larger mesh, 7½ inches, since it was near the bottom so it was unlikely that the salmon would venture that deep to escape.

Once the web was dried, it took about a week to construct the net. All the crew participated, each man having a specific skill in the constructing of the purse seine. In my early years, my job was simply filling the needles and it was a chore just to keep up, as each job required a different strength of twine. Eventually I graduated to become a skilled web man thanks to my Uncle Tony who was a real expert with a needle. My cousin Don Francin and I would race to see how fast we could finish one pull. A pull was about 10 fathoms of net. There was always a bit of fun in the competition.

Each Sunday afternoon, once the season began, we left Anacortes for the fishing grounds. I distinctly remember my first trip out as a cabin boy. I was awfully proud of myself as I threw my brand new sea bag and hip boots aboard the Veribus just like the men did. I learned early on that you are never late for a sailing. I never was and most of the time I was aboard before anyone else showed up. Yet, I remember pulling out from the slip into the waterway as some tardy sailor came running down the ramp flaying his arms to no avail.

From Anacortes it was about two hours to the protected bay (often we anchored up in Biz Point on the southwest side of Fidalgo Island) where we dropped anchor for the night. My grandfather selected a location close to where the tides would be the most favorable the next morning when the season opened.

I remember lying on deck, as the wind blew through my hair, watching the bow cut sharply through the icy, blue salt water. This is when my love affair with the sea began and it has never ended. Occasionally, a family of porpoise caught up with us and played off the bow, diving and swirling around for hours. It was a splendid time to build memories and fantasize about the future.

The season in those days was regulated by the Washington State Fish and Game Department. The weekly opening started at 6 a.m. Monday and ended at 6 p.m. on Friday. At the closing on Friday each crewman was given a fish to take home to his family. I remember us cleaning the salmon on the after deck and throwing the offal over the side, where dozens of seagulls would dive into the water to capture their dinner.

In Puget Sound the salmon season started in mid-May with a short King salmon season, and ended about Thanksgiving time when the last dog (chum) salmon was harvested. My season started the first day school was let out and ended the first day school started. By early September, I was ready to go back to school and tell friends about my summer adventures.

In the winter I often went down to the boat with my grandfather who checked on his precious Veribus daily and pumped out any water that accumulated in the bilge. As he became ill, I willingly took over that task along with doing my Seattle Times paper route.

I was sort of a street kid living right down in the village. I had a variety of jobs up and down Commercial Avenue, including washing windows for a dozen or so merchants, sweeping the garage at the bus depot, and dusting Bill Affleck's handsome 1952 burgundy-colored Fleetwood Sedan Cadillac.

When I started seventh grade, Carl Swartze asked me to come to work at Northern Supply Company, which sold war surplus stock. It later became Carl's Men Store. I did stocking, cleaning, and soon became a junior salesman. Carl was a terrific guy to work for. He was a veteran of the Second World War where he had been an infantryman. While being transported in a glider he was in a dreadful crash and nearly died. He ended up with a steel plate in his head. Often he would have horrendous headaches and occasionally a seizure and fall to the floor. I must say that the first time that occurred I was pretty frightened.

My other interesting "kid job" was babysitting for Ralph and Jean Bryson who owned the mortuary and ambulance service. They had three little girls and on Saturday night when they went out I babysat. When an accident occurred or when someone died they would rush home. Jean would take over watching the girls and off I would go with Ralph.

If we took the ambulance I sat in the rear of the vehicle in a jump seat. When we took the hearse I sat up front with Ralph. If Ralph wasn't available, I would accompany Mike Casper who operated the skating rink as his day job. Either way, they were eye-opening experiences and certainly, at a very young age, taught me the value of human life. It was the first time I thought about my mortality and how precious each day is. The most traumatic event was cutting down a corpse that had been hanging on a rope from a tree out near Heart Lake for way too long.

The other incident I well remember was a severe accident in 1954 out near Lake Campbell. It was one of the first years of the new panoramic windshields. Three drunken sailors from the Whidbey Island Airbase didn't make a sharp curve in their new Ford and all three flew through the windshield. The sailor we picked up was in a very life-threatening condition. His leg was nearly severed. Someone hurriedly put a tourniquet on it and off we sped to a hospital. The nerves in the leg were causing the leg to severely spasm. I had to lie over it so it didn't cause even more damage. I don't know what ever happened to that sailor. Did he live, keep his leg, was it amputated, or did he die? I still think about that kid who at the time was no more than twenty years of age. So often in life we meet someone in the most unusual circumstances never to see them again.

In those years, 1948-1953, we fished around the San Juan Islands at Iceberg Point, Cattle Point, the Lime Kiln, James Island, Strawberry Bay, the south side of Lummi Island, and the Rosario Straits. However, Grandpa's favorite spots were Rosario Beach, around Deception Island and down along West Beach on Whidbey Island.

Each morning we arose at 4 a.m. lifted anchor and headed out for the fishing grounds. The cook would have the coffee brewing and would lay out fruit and rolls. I didn't drink coffee so the cook would often make me hot chocolate. I remember the men pouring a heavy dose of evaporated milk in their coffee.

Our first set (the laying out of the net) in the morning was often at a familiar location where the tide expectantly would be just right. Grandpa carefully watched the kelp and the white foam curled up against the rocks. When it would turn seaward he positioned the boat to make the set. It was often just nearing daybreak, as seldom do you catch fish in the dark. After we pulled in the net and if the tide had changed we would run at full throttle to another location hoping to again catch the tide at its prime.

While we ran we would enjoy a hearty breakfast of ham, sausage, bacon and eggs, pancakes or French toast. Breakfast was an important meal because if the fishing was heavy you may not be able to eat the rest of the day other than having a sandwich thrown at you.

I learned early on that you didn't have to see signs of fish such as jumpers or finners to catch fish. If you knew the tides, and if the fish were running, you would catch them. I remember clearly Grandpa's patience in waiting for the prime time to set the net. It was a key to his success. Patience and planning have been key factors throughout my life.

Jumpers are fish that fling themselves out of the water, sometimes jumping just once or several times. Each species of salmon has its own style of jumping, and an experienced fisherman can tell which species it is from a far distance. It was generally held that you could catch about 1,000 fish for each jumper you saw. It was important that all crewmen including the cook and engineer watch carefully for fish. I watched religiously and after a few years could see fish hundreds of yards away. It just took patience, perseverance, and a sharp pair of eyes.

Finners are groups of fish whose dorsal fins barely break the surface of the water. It is very difficult to see finners, especially if there is any wind or chop on the sea.

Weather permitting we made eight to ten sets a day. A set is the releasing of the net into the sea, holding it open for approximately twenty minutes and then pulling it back in, hoping it is full of sleek blue-back salmon. It took about one and one-half hours to complete a set. In those days prior to the invention of the power block the net was hauled in by hand. It was especially difficult and back breaking when the wind was blowing or the tide was pulling against the net. We would generally finish up our day between 8:00 and 10:00 p.m.

After the fishing day, we would locate a tender boat to pitch up and to sell our catch. A tender is a vessel that buys fish from the catcher vessels (like the Veribus) and then delivers them to a particular cannery. We always sold to the Sebastian Stuart Fish Company so we had to find one of its tenders which would be anchored up in a protected bay. For many years our designated tender was either the Gertrude S or the Evelyn S. Each evening one of them would call us on the radio phone to advise us of her location. If there were boats lined up ahead of us and if they had large catches it could take several hours to unload and clean up the boat. Often the crew took a quick snooze while waiting for our turn to pitch up.

My grandpa had a friend who owned the tender Cutty Sark. The first time my grandmother met his friend's wife, she said, "It is a pleasure to meet you, Mrs. Veribus." My grandmother, without hesitation, said, "And it is a pleasure to meet you as well, Mrs. Cutty Sark."

In the spring and summer, most of the salmon we caught were Sockeye with a smattering of King and Coho (Silvers). As fall arrived, the Sockeye diminished in quantity, and more and more Chums and Pinks appeared with a token increase in Coho. On the odd years—1949, 1951 and '53—there was a run of Pink salmon (humpies), as well. Since there were huge runs of Pinks in Alaska, the price for Puget Sound Pinks was dismal.

Our days were long and tiring and when fish were plentiful the days got even longer. Yet, when the fish were abundant the crew didn't tire as it did when we would drag set after set for barely any catch. The first couple of years, I didn't always quite make the 4 a.m. wakeup call from the skipper when he called down into the fo'c's'le with a simple, "Okay, boys." I remember the engine's oily smell and the odor of a bunch of fishermen at that time in the morning. It was certainly refreshing to get up on deck and take in the fresh salt air.

The first two years, my chores on the Veribus included cleaning my grandfather's cabin; washing the never-ending supply of dishes, pots and pans and scrubbing the galley deck to the point of spotlessness. Yet, my favorite time was on the bridge sitting at my grandfather's left side listening to the stories of the old country (now Croatia) and learning the traditions of the sea. Little by little, over the six summers that I sailed with him I learned to steer, operate the throttle and gears, and how to navigate by compass. Slowly I began to understand the signs of the sea and I asked a million questions. I worshipped my grandfather, and looking back I think it was mutual.

Grandpa thought since I could run the boat that I should also be able to drive his car and I did starting at about age 12. He had this great old 1948 Dodge Sedan that appeared huge to me, and it was. He had to put a pillow under my rear so I could see through the windshield.

I remember predominantly his stories about his hometown of Vela Luka, another island community thousands of miles away in old Europe. Nearly 35 years later, my son John and I visited Vela Luka and the surrounding area and saw for ourselves the similarities between it and that of the San Juan Islands. Immediately, I understood why the Croatian community settled in northwestern Washington. Vela Luka is situated on the western side of the island of Korcula in Croatia, in a bay filled with many tiny islets. The area has a mild Adriatic-type climate, unpolluted sea and air, and groves of fig and olive trees. The nights are clear with a rich perfume emanating from the many pine trees. The walking path around the Vela Luka Bay was just as my grandfather described. I envisioned his family walking in this place just as John and I were doing. The beauty and serenity as he described it had not changed.

There were also many small fishing boats moored along the quay unloading their catches of octopi, mackerel, and shrimp. It is an incredibly picturesque island, similar to Fidalgo Island where Anacortes is located.

When we arrived in Split, Croatia, we immediately noticed how many tall men there were and the many basketball hoops scattered about the city. In the last few years many Croatian ball players have been playing in the NBA and on major European club teams.

We also enjoyed abundant meals of fresh seafood. Many of the recipes were recognizable and delicious. The Croats love their seafood and their basketball.

The most noticeable event on our trip was the inflation. The Croatian Kùna (HRK) was dropping like a rock. Each time we exchanged our U.S. dollars for Kunas, we received double of what we had just a few days earlier. We literally had to get a small gym bag to carry our currency. It was similar to the hyperinflation of the Deutsche mark just after the First World War. It was a frightening time for the Croatian citizens and a precursor to what was to come.

We also visited the museum of Ivan Mestrovic, the renowned Croatian sculptor. He was lauded by Rodin as "the greatest phenomenon amongst the sculptors." His work is featured in museums around the world. We tried purchasing a small piece offered by an art gallery; however we learned it was illegal to take any of Mestrovic's art out of the country.

My grandfather came to the United States from Croatia, which at that time was part of the Austrian-Hungarian Empire. His passport shows that he arrived at Ellis Island on May 10, 1906. He was 25 years of age, having been born on February 28, 1881. Upon reaching the New World, he traveled to Minnesota to work in the coal mines. When he saved enough money, he sent for his wife, Palma Separovich Tasovac, and daughter Eva. They arrived at Ellis Island in June of 1911 and made the transcontinental journey to Anacortes by train. Grandfather had purchased a piece of property on 15th Street in Anacortes and constructed a small temporary dwelling. Soon thereafter, he built a two-story four-bedroom house where my grandmother gave birth to two more daughters: Pauline in 1913 and my mother, Helen Violet, on May 17,

John Tasovac family in 1917. From left to right: Helen, John, Pauline, Palma and Eva.

9

1914. It was a cozy home surrounded by apple trees and a large vegetable garden, which my grandmother tended.

I remember the numerous Sunday family dinners at that house. The meal always started with a macaroni dish followed by a main entrée of chicken or beef. Sunday was a meat day while weekday meals were often comprised of a fish dish. We always had zayah as well, and the recipe is featured in the recipe section at the end of the book.

It was a time before television, and after dinner the adults talked and the kids went outside to play. It was always a favorite adventure to explore grandfather's wine cellar where barrels of wine were aging. I remember the earthy aromas coming from the wines' fermentation.

I also treasure the memories of sitting on my grandfather's knee in late summer enjoying one of maybe six figs that matured on his well-nurtured fig tree. It was planted right outside the back door where it received southern exposure. I have planted three fig trees at our home in Port Townsend, and we have had plentiful harvests on two of the three trees. Fig trees are meant to be grown in a Mediterranean-type climate, which is certainly not found in the Puget Sound area; yet besides the luscious fruit, the 10- to 12-foot deciduous palmate leaves are both attractive and provide great shade. In the summer of 2011 we harvested over 100 mature figs.

When my grandson Miles visited one autumn, I tried to share a fig with him. He wanted no part of it. It is a truism that we can't relive our memories, no matter how much we treasured them.

There have been several Croatian settlements in Washington. A small Croatian fishing village existed in the beginning of the 19th century, where experienced Croatian fishermen contributed to the development of the fishing industry. The main Croatian centers in Washington were Seattle, Tacoma, Everett, Anacortes and Roslyn.

Commercial fishing in the 1940s and '50s was an incredible experience for a young boy. I recall to this day the chug-a chug-a-chuga of the Veribus' Atlas diesel engine, the smell of the freshly caught salmon being brailed out of the net, the sound of dropping anchor, hearing the clankety-clank clatter of the chain flying out and the rush in the crew when the captain screamed "Let her go!"—A term that commanded the crew to release the net into the sea.

My grandfather had mostly crew members his age (in their 60s), and they were patient, old guys who loved to spin yarns and teach me how to patch net, splice lines, read tide books, and to throw a bucket over the side to fetch water and not lose the bucket.

Those were different times, when life was slow and easy, and the life of a fisherman was conducive to building long and enduring relationships. Many of the crew had worked together for several years and built life long bonds. We had hours on board traveling from one fishing location to another. It was also a time when I appreciated the harsh beauty of the sea. I learned at an early age to have an unrelenting respect for the sea despite its masquerades. The tides and currents of Puget Sound are worthy of the highest respect.

Over the years when I returned to Anacortes I often visited the men that I fished with and many of whom were in declining health. I understood how fleeting life is, as I saw those once powerful and hearty men dying an often long and painful death. I recently visited one of the skippers with whom I fished. He was a great athlete, a decorated naval officer, and a man who always took good care of himself. When I last visited him after a stroke, he was seated around a table at an assisted-living center with three women who were suffering from Alzheimer's disease. My friend recognized me and gave me his best smile with his bright eyes. He made my day.

In the 1940's and 50's many people in Anacortes were engaged in the harvest and processing of the salmon. Housewives, school kids and teachers all secured summer jobs at the local canneries. Others found jobs on fishing or tender boats. Anyone who wanted to work could work. Those were post-depression times and many people were struggling financially. Yet, few complained. During the peak of the season the canneries operated 24 hours a day seven days a week. There were five canneries on the Anacortes waterfront which included Fisherman Packing Corporation, American Packing, Carroll's Cannery, Farwest Fisheries, and Sebastian Stuart Fish Company.

On most weekends there were as many as 200 purse seiners tied up at the various docks in Anacortes. This meant there were nearly 1,600 men in town. All of this activity generated income for the fuel docks, hardware and marine supply stores, clothing stores, restaurants, and bars. Still the stores that benefited the most were the grocery stores, and none more than Luvera's Market. Today Luvera's would be classified as a superior gourmet market. In those days it was dearly appreciated and nearly every Croatian boat's cook shopped there for his groceries and meat including olive oil, salami, seasonal fruits and vegetables and their outstanding French bread. My grandfather said, "You can't make a season by skimping on the grub bill" and he certainly never did. I remember particularly the crates of peaches, grapes and strawberries that would always be in the larder on the upper deck.

Luvera's hired dozens of workers to prepare the huge grocery orders on Friday and Saturday. Then early on Sunday morning they delivered to the docks and loaded everything onto the boats' deck. It was a herculean management challenge and the Luvera's were always up to it. Paul Luvera Sr. later became a state senator and after retirement carved totem poles and then grandfather clocks. I have a Luvera 15 foot totem overseeing Puget Sound from the backyard of my mother's home in Anacortes. It has five templates, each one chosen by a member of our family. They include a salmon, of course, an eagle, bear, raven and wolf.

Often on Friday nights when the boats were in port there were street dances with live bands. This definitely livened up the village. I am not so sure how some of the more conservative town folk felt about the rowdiness of those Friday nights but one thing was for sure, everyone appreciated the economic impact that the fleet created on those weekends.

In the mid-1990s one of my favorite old fisherman friends, Charlie Greenwood, then in his 90's and residing in an assisted-living facility, asked his son to call me. Charlie wanted to see me. I hadn't seen Charlie for over 25 years. He was from Lopez Island and had fished with my grandfather to help pay the real estate taxes on his farm. We went for a drive and I expressed to him how much I appreciated all he had taught me. He told me that the Lopez Island property that he was barely able to hold on to back in the 1950s was now worth a few million dollars. He knew that at his age he wouldn't get much enjoyment from his new-found wealth. He said how strange life was and that he never looked too far ahead but lived his life one day at a time. Charlie died a few weeks later.

Through the years I saw my grandfather; this imposing yet kind and patient man deteriorate in health as a result of prostate cancer. He suffered incredibly from that dreadful disease. I remember taking the bus from Anacortes on Sundays to visit him at Virginia Mason Hospital in Seattle. I was only 10 or so but my mother worked for the local bus company so the driver, I suspect, kept an eye on me.

In 1954, after enduring enormous pain over several years grandpa turned the wheel of the Veribus over to my uncle, his son-in-law, Tony Francin. It was the most difficult decision he ever made. I continued fishing on the Veribus with Tony for the next two summers. At age 14, I was no longer the flunky cabin boy, but a full-fledged deck hand. My uncle was a tough taskmaster yet in looking back his sternness certainly didn't hurt me.

Tony was an amazing net man. He was known throughout the fleet as the fastest man with a needle. I remember him making these 4 foot long decorative fenders out of 2-inch manila rope that were like pieces of art. I grew in size and maturity those two summers under the influence of Uncle Tony.

In Tony's first year as skipper, Puget Sound produced one of the largest sockeye salmon runs in its history. We loaded down ("plugged the boat") the Veribus twice that season with well over 10,000 blood-red sockeye each time. One of these whopping sets was at Point Roberts near the Canadian boundary line and the other was on the famous Salmon Banks off San Juan Island. It is difficult to express the emotion of seeing a net full of these magnificent Sockeye thrashing about in the white Sea. In all the years that I would fish I would never see this poignant sight again.

My grandfather had come out with us the week we made one of those big sets and in all his exuberance while helping to pull up the bunt (the heavy webbing at the end of the net), he nearly fell overboard. He was pretty embarrassed.

The average weight of a Sockeye was 7½ pounds and at a going market price of 25 cents per pound it was a banner season. In those days each crewman received a share of the cash value of the catch. On the Veribus we had eight crewmen and each received one share. The captain, the boat owner and the net owner each received two shares for a total of 14. The share to each crewman for that one day when we caught the 10,000 Sockeye amounted to approximately $1,500.00. In 2010 dollars that would be nearly $15,000.00. It was an enormous amount of money for a 14-year-old kid in 1954, and it wouldn't be too bad today either.

I took home a very big paycheck that season and after buying some school clothes we remodeled our kitchen with a new electric stove, refrigerator, hot water tank, and a washer and dryer. And after all that I still had a few dollars for my savings account that my grandfather started for me the first year I began fishing.

The next year 1955 was a virtual bust, the antithesis of 1954. I learned quickly that such is the game of commercial fishing. Nevertheless I continued to become more proficient at mending nets, splicing cable and rope. I acquired a deeper understanding of the problematical ways of the sea. Despite how bad that season turned out, we did make wages and I had no complaints. However, I came to realize how financially difficult those bad years were for crewmen who were married and raising a family. Many depended on their summer crew shares, but with declining runs that changed and many fishermen headed to Alaska to participate in the King crab rush.

CHAPTER TWO

ALASKA

ONE WINTER EVENING IN 1956, Francis Barcott, a top Anacortes skipper called my mother to ask her if I could go as a deckhand with him to Alaska on the F/V Cypress.

I remember she said, "Ask Gary. His decision will be all right with me." That was how my mother, a single mom operated. I took the phone and told Francis that I would enjoy sailing with him and that I really appreciate the chance. It was the start of a long and gratifying relationship.

On Father's Day of 1956 we departed Anacortes and I made my first voyage up the Inland Passage to Southeast Alaska. As we pulled out from the port dock the wharf was filled with friends, family and well-wishers. When the boats started their engines the captains and crew members embraced their lovers and wives. Hardy handshakes were given to old and new friends alike. My mother, family members and many friends were there to see us off. I felt a smidgen of a twang as our boat pulled out into Guemes Channel, our steamboat type whistles blared and all arms waved frantically.

As we headed west, the crisp blue sea was whipsawed by a southerly wind causing the tips of the waves to become sharp and white. I never dreamed I would spend the next 36 years in Alaska in the commercial fishing business.

The trip north to Alaska from Puget Sound is truly one of the world's most enchanting sea voyages. God's beauty is not any more revealed than it is along the inside passage through British Columbia to Alaska. We headed up Georgia Straits through Active Pass and Discovery Passage to Seymour Narrows,

Seymour Narrows

where the tides were monumental. I had heard for years the stories of how Seymour Narrows, north of Campbell River, was one of the most treacherous areas for mariners in all of North America. When I first made this trip Ripple Rock, located in the center of Seymour Narrows, was a navigator's nightmare. At its maximum the tide ran at 14 knots. The tide books advised to only go through the Narrows at slack water. However, our caravan of seiners, the St. Bernadette, Dora R, Souvenir and the Cypress slid up the eastern shore so close to the rocks that I felt we could touch them.

Two years later, on April 5, 1958, after 27 months of around-the-clock work at a cost in excess of $3.1 million, Ripple Rock was blown out of the water. It was the largest non-nuclear explosion ever. The blast pulverized 370,000 tons of rock and displaced 320,000 tons of water. The rock and debris rocketed over 1,000 feet into the air. The explosion also created a 25-foot tidal wave, which quickly dissipated and caused no damage. They accomplished this feat by constructing a 570-foot vertical shaft at Maud Island, a 2,500-foot stretch of tunnel under the ocean floor and placed 300 ton of explosives into the two 300-foot vertical raises into each tooth of Ripple Rock. The demolition operation was a complete success. The undersea hazard had finally been conquered.

Seymour Narrows

St. Bernadette in Seymour Narrows

Campbell River

The Princess Patricia in the Inside Passage

18

Lighthouse along the Inside Passage

Seiners working near North Inian Island

It was an immense blessing for navigators.

Leaving the Narrows we soon entered Johnstone Strait which is nearly 60 miles long with countless resplendent waterfalls all along this stretch of Vancouver Island. Many of these waterfalls plummeted over 150 feet. We then moved into Broughton Strait, Queen Charlotte Sound and Fitzhugh Sound. I enjoyed learning the curious names of the buoys, lights, fog signals and radio beacons such as: Sea Egg Rocks, Cinque Islands, Ripple Shoal Buoy, Broken Island Light, Scarlett Point Light, Cape Caution Light, Fog Rocks Light, Bella Bella Lights, Elephant Head, Lawyer Islands, Hog Rocks and many, many more. All seemed to have sing-song names that were easy to memorize.

From Fitzhugh Sound we proceeded through Lama Passage to Seaforth Channel across Millbank Sound to Finlayson Channel. We then headed to Tolmie Sound and through Graham Reach to Fraser Reach and into Wright Sound. From there we followed Grenville Channel for over 40 miles. At this point we were only about 100 miles from Ketchikan. We passed Lawyer Island and moved into Chatham Sound followed by Holiday Passage and Dixon Entrance, the last open body of water. As we passed Tree Point Light and before long we were in Revillagigedo Channel and Ketchikan. We landed at the Standard Oil dock.

On our voyage we ran 24 hours a day and Ketchikan was the first stop. Those many hours traveling provided time to read, play cribbage or just appreciate the amazing country. I loved to read and with the foresight of Ms. Brinkley, the Anacortes librarian, I was supplied with a summer's stockpile of great reading. Each summer she packed me a crate of books which included some classics as well as some great reads for a young boy. By the time I entered Santa Clara University I had read a considerable number of the classics. I will always appreciate and never forget the impact that Ms. Brinkley had on my life.

We fueled up in Ketchikan, took on water and purchased a few groceries that were overlooked in Anacortes. Leaving Ketchikan we sailed to Wrangell where there was a Farwest Cannery. We stopped to take our net out of the hold where it was stored for the trip north. The Canadian authorities do not allow American fishing vessels to have their gear on deck while passing through their waters.

That first summer in Wrangell I was down in the hold helping to clear the net as it was being hauled up on deck. The skipper yelled down to me that a young woman was asking for me. As I looked upon the dock I saw a very pregnant Indian girl glaring down at me. She shouted out as she saw me, "That's not the Gary I'm looking for!" I believe there were a few expletives thrown in as well. Needless to say, I was razzed about that for years to come.

Leaving Wrangell we entered Wrangell Narrows, a winding, 22 mile channel between Mitkof Island and Kupreanof Island in the Alexander Archipelago in Southeast Alaska. There are about 60 navigational lights and buoys to mark the channel because of its winding nature and the accompanying hazards. It was named Wrangell Strait in 1838 after Admiral Baron Ferdinand Petrovich von Wrangell.

The town of Petersburg is at the north end of the Narrows. The Narrows opens up to Frederick Sound to the north and Sumner Strait to the south. We sometime stopped in Petersburg which is often referred to as Alaska's Little Norway. It was founded more than 100 years ago by Norwegian fishermen. It was named after Peter Buschmann, a Norwegian immigrant who arrived in the late 1890s and homesteaded on the north end of Mitkof Island. He built a cannery, sawmill and a dock in the late 1800s. His family's homesteads grew into Petersburg, which was populated largely by people of Scandinavian origin. The cannery has operated continuously since its completion. Petersburg is one of Alaska's major fishing communities with many of Southeast Alaska's highline fishermen residing there.

Leaving Petersburg, we proceeded through Frederick Sound and into Chatham Straits followed by Icy Straits and finally into the Inian Islands and to Elfin Cove. We headquartered in Elfin Cove through the end of July, when we moved down to Noyes Island. Elfin Cove is a tiny jewel of an inlet located just south of Cape Spencer the last point of civilization before sailors began their the journey across the treacherous Gulf of Alaska.

As we passed Point Adolphus in Icy Straits I noticed a great clamoring in the water and at a closer watch I saw several humpback whales propelling themselves out of the water. As they crashed back it created a huge splatter. We moved closer to this exhibition and I could see their sleek black heads

Inian Islands

Icy Straits

22

Icebergs in Icy Straits

The St. Bernadette

and the molted black and white on their ventral side. As they thrust upward they exposed their patterned underside, unique to each whale. The humpback ranges from 40 to 50 feet in length and weighs about 50 tons. They are very acrobatic and engaged in tail lobbing (raising their flukes out of the water and pounding it on the surface) and flipper slapping (using their flippers to slap the water). It is thought that these acts are a means of communication between the humpbacks. I learned that these whales arrived every June to feed and perform this aerial spectacle. After that phenomenal visual experience, I kept a close eye whenever we passed by Point Adolphus. It turned out to be a fantastic place to watch humpback whales, sea lions, bald eagles, great flocks of seagulls, and even the odd grizzly bear fishing on the beach.

Further west was Elfin Cove one of the most picturesque locations in all of Alaska. It was located on the northern shore of Chichagof Island. A narrow canal ran from the sea side of the cove into an inner harbor which opened up into a wondrous emerald bay watched over by jagged, snowcapped mountains.

We tied up for the weekends inside the flask-shaped harbor. There wasn't much there other than an old-time general store and Standard Oil fuel station owned by Ruth and Ernest Swanson and a post office and liquor shack operated by a woman whose name now escapes me. Ernie built the dock, the store and a restaurant in the 1920s. At that time the harbor went by the name "Gunk Hole." When he married Ruth, she applied to be the postmistress but refused to apply for "Gunk Hole" and had the name changed to Elfin Cove, after Ernie's fishing boat, the Elfin.

The Swanson's came to be cherished friends. Each summer they opened up the lower floor of their home to the fishermen to play cards, read or just enjoy a lively conversation. They also generously built a shower room for the fishermen to use at no charge. My friend Paul Luvera Jr. and I played chess in the comfortable room on those long rainy weekends after taking a hot shower.

The Swanson's also provided the fireworks for the Fourth of July. For several years, I was the official pyrotechnic handler. The 4th was a major celebration in Alaska, as it was the only holiday when the weather was halfway decent. The old gal at the liquor store had her biggest payday of the year and invariably ran out of inventory to the disappointment of the thirsty seamen.

Elfin Cove

Inian Islands

25

Looking north from Inian Islands

Bill Sims, Mike McGreevy and friend, churning ice cream

Week end net repairs in Elfin Cove

Fred Knapp doing a little wash

On weekends friends and I would take the skiff and explore the nearby islands. Many were populated with red, grey, white, and blue fox from the days that the Russians owned Alaska and raised them for their pelts. One of these islands was a military installation during the Second World War and cannons still remained facing the Gulf where all enemy ships had to pass by in order to reach the inland waters.

Those summers that I sailed with Francis Barcott were memorable experiences. The "Skipper" was a man's man, an individualist who always said things straight up. He never minced words and everyone always knew how they stood with F.B. He was patriotic, political, worshipped his wife Ethel, his children and his God. What's more, he was a highline fisherman who knew his trade as well as any skipper in the fleet. He was a true master of the sea.

He also was a gourmand and exceptional cook. I learned how to cook and to enjoy cooking while fishing with F.B. There was never anything dull about the food we enjoyed aboard the F/V Cypress. On the weekends the food on the galley table ranged from seaweed salads to sautéed octopus, which required par boiling, skinning, and then pounding the ivory-white meat to a light, tasty texture. When we were laid up waiting out a storm, F.B. would take over the galley and would prepare sumptuous soups, fresh-fried clams and a marvelous San Francisco-style Crab Cioppino.

Francis died October 31, 1995, doing what he loved, skippering a purse seiner. He was fishing for "dogs" (chum salmon) in Hood Canal when he suffered a heart attack. He is buried at Grandview Cemetery in Anacortes with a picture of his boat, Ethel B, engraved on his tombstone. I heard F.B. often say "I am a salmon fisherman; it's what I am."

Going ashore to pick fresh, wild strawberries and blueberries on Lemesurier Island, a small island in Icy Straits was a highlight of the season. An elderly couple lived on the island and made their income as fishing and hunting guides. They were proud of their famous guests who included film stars Gary Cooper and Clark Gable. They also maintained an outstanding vegetable garden. In the summer, when the sun was out nearly 20 hours a day and the growing season was 100 days long they were able to grow copious quantities of produce for their winter larder. Their vegetables including cabbage, rutabagas, carrots, turnips, and potatoes, were huge. They explained to me that in the Matanuska Valley, near Fairbanks, these same vegetables grew to record size including cabbage that weighed in at over 60 pounds. I don't think I exactly believed them until years later when I visited the Matanuska Valley and saw these giant vegetables myself.

As with all life's experiences there were down sides. The most notable were the times when the web (the netting) got tangled around the rudder post and the wheel (the propeller). This generally occurred when there were gusting winds and the skiff was unable to tow the seiner away from the cork line. When this happened the entanglement had to be cleared before the engine could be put in gear. Otherwise, the wheel simply wrapped the lines and webbing tightly around the shaft and would render the vessel powerless. This could cause serious problems and put lives at risk. So, as tradition had it, the youngest crewman was elected to strip down, dive overboard, swim down and clear the obstruction. I did this several times and I usually could do it quickly. However, one time in Icy Straits it was not an easy fix. The web was firmly wrapped around the propeller and I wasn't able to loosen it. I came up for air several times until finally I had to cut the webbing off. This required a considerable amount of time. When they pulled me back up after several minutes I was seriously hypothermic. Some crew members took me to my bunk, loaded on blankets, and fed me hot liquids. It was several hours later before I finally stopped shivering and came out of my delirium. It was terrifying. When I started skippering my own boat the first item I purchased and brought aboard was a wet suit. We used it often, too often.

When we left Icy Straits we headed for Noyes Island and Steamboat Bay. It was a very appealing area for the seine fleet because most of the salmon caught in southeast Alaska were Pink salmon the lowest valued salmon used almost exclusively for canning. However, around Noyes Island there was also a sizeable run of Canadian-bound Sockeye that passed through the area bound for the Frazer River. They amounted to nearly 20% of the catch and their value was five times that of the lowly Pink. Fishing off Noyes Island was not easy. In fact, it was the most treacherous fishing area in Southeast Alaska.

The fishing grounds were located just off of Cape Ulitka in the North

Pacific Ocean. Every time we turned the corner at the Cape the crew made certain everything was tightly battened down. Many times we had to hold up in Ulitka Bay, as the waves were so high we couldn't safely negotiate the turn out to the fishing grounds. I played many a game of cribbage in Ulitka Bay where we spent numerous hours and sometimes days.

My first year with F.B., I was the skipper of the skiff. At Noyes Island the swells were often so high that from the time the crew released the skiff (the weight of which pulled the net off of the platform on the stern) and we began towing the net (keeping it open for the fish to enter), we didn't see the seiner again until we began towing the net back toward her. It was dangerous fishing and I had to keep fully concentrated on the moment, as a mental error could cost someone their life. I was a sixteen year old kid but I had been around the fishing game long enough to realize the consequences and I was dead serious when we fished in those waters.

One day, I was towing away when I saw a williwaw (a sudden violent wind) coming our way. It appeared as if it were viciously dancing across the sea without a clear direction. I knew if it passed through us we would capsize. It was not meant to be, conversely the Libby #12 was not so fortunate. The williwaw hit that old seiner broadside and knocked her over in 10 seconds flat. Providentially another big swell set her back up. She was through for the season, as her engine room filled with water, but remarkably no lives were lost. Noyes Island was no place for the faint of heart.

We spent our weekends in Steamboat Bay. It was about five miles from the Cape and was a protected anchorage. Steamboat Bay had been one of the largest canneries in Alaska. It was operated by the New England Fish Company. They obtained most of their supply from a fish trap on Cape Ulitka. Now it was simply a place to tie up, repair and store nets and do laundry. It also had a commissary and a large bank of hot showers. Some elite skippers spent their whole season in this fishing area. I remember George Hamilton, one of the fleets preeminent purse seine skippers rolling into the Bay at full throttle blowing his whistle with a broom tied to the top of the mast. This was a proud indicator that they had caught 100,000 fish. George hit that mark nearly every season hauling at a location called the Haystack, a treacherous place where nets were often lost. Skippers had to grasp each area thoroughly and be able to lay out their nets knowing confidently that they could retrieve them safely. Losing or "tearing up" a net was not only costly but took precious time to rebuild or repair, time that you may not have. We never knew when the fish would disappear from an area. Often we would be into heavy fishing one day only to find the fish entirely gone the next.

As a young skipper I learned a costly lesson. We were into heavy fishing on the west end of Lemesurier Island in Icy Straits. There was not another boat around. At mid-day our hatch was over half full. I thought if I were to run and deliver to the tender I would have an empty hatch and could fill her up on the next tide. It didn't happen. When we got back to the fishing grounds there was not a fish to be seen let alone to be caught. It was a lifelong object lesson.

Every Friday night in Steamboat Bay I went to the commissary and purchased a number 10 tin of canned apricots and headed to the shower. It was my weekly reward to myself. Another benefit of fishing in these remote areas was that you couldn't spend your money easily.

I said that Steamboat was a good moorage and it was most of the time. However, one night we were tethered up with five other seiners. I suppose now that there may have been only one anchor out. And as it often happens in Alaska the weather changed unexpectedly. The wind came up so ferociously that it moved the tethered boats out towards the sea. Fortunately Captain Rudolph Franulovich of the St. Bernadette woke up and sounded the alarm. Everyone rushed to start their engines and all turned out favorably. I say fortunately because the tide and wind had carried us within about 50 yards of a treacherous reef.

One early morning in August of 1956 I was picking blueberries off of an abandoned fish scow at the head of Steamboat Bay. Glancing up I saw some terrifying visitors. There gazing at me were a pair of gray wolves, baring their yellowish teeth while emitting deep guttural growls. I dropped the nearly full bucket of berries, dove in the icy bay and swam to the boat thinking that I was safe. A few days later we were sailing across the bay and witnessed a pack of wolves swimming from one island to another. Wolves can swim too.

The experiences aboard the F/V Cypress were exciting times. We fished in challenging storms, caught huge amounts of salmon and worked until we thought we would drop. Yet, I enjoyed each day inhaling the vast splendor of Alaska.

I remember clearly those colorful men I sailed with. Many had served in the Second World War and had grueling experiences that they sometimes shared. In retrospect I suspect they told me very little. One shipmate had been a tank commander whose unit was ambushed and all his comrades were killed except for him. He had horrible nightmares and sometimes would curl up in a corner trembling. He didn't tell me what had occurred; I learned it from his son many years later after he had passed away. I can still see the agony in his face. I learned early on from my mother not to judge others precipitously and these experiences only reinforced that solid advice.

Men came from all over the country wanting to try their luck at fishing as it was a chance to hit it big in a few short weeks. There were always stories floating around about the incredible amount of money that could be made and it was true in some instances. Yet like many things in life and in business, we hear what we want or wish to be true. The minimum wage in 1955 was $1.00 so the thought of a big payday drew men from all walks of life. Some that I knew were meat cutters, loggers, teachers, tanker crewmen, cooks, bartenders, and cedar shake makers. They all had a story and I listened intently and learned from their life experiences.

On the evening of July 7, 1958, we were anchored up in South Inian Cove after pitching up our day's catch to the tender. I was in a top bunk on the port side of the boat near the bow. Suddenly I felt the boat moving up and down in a most unfamiliar way. I lifted myself up through the skylight and looked upon the mountain where vast numbers of trees were tumbling down. I jumped up yelling, started the engine and ran up the ladder to the foredeck where I hauled in the anchor and all in about three minutes. Quickly we moved out of the Cove and free from the peril. We soon learned that a magnitude 8.0 earthquake had struck along the Fairweather Fault. It had caused a large landside at the head of Lityua Bay some 20 miles from where we were anchored. Lityua Bay is located off the Gulf of Alaska and within the Glacier Bay National Park. The quake caused a tsunami of frightening size. The massive rockslide caused water to surge about 1800 feet generating what is called a gravity wave. This wave swept out of the bay carrying with it a troller that was anchored in Anchor Cove. It was carried in front of the largest wave crest and those onboard estimated they cleared La Chaussee Spit (at the mouth of Lituya Bay) by 100 feet or more. I learned later it had landed upside down on its main cabin which was constructed from 1½ inch marine-grade plywood.

A young couple that I had met in Elfin Cove also vanished after being caught in the gigantic wave. I had just talked with them the previous weekend when they told me this was going to be their last summer trolling, as they had saved enough money to buy a farm up in the Matanuska Valley. Three women were also killed while picking wild strawberries as the north end of Khantaak Island when it slipped into the sea. This major earthquake was felt over a large area of Southeast Alaska, as far south as Seattle and east to Whitehorse, Yukon Territory, Canada.

The week following the earthquake there were no salmon to be caught. The murky glacier water lacked oxygen and the salmon had moved on. What we hauled up were the most unusual species of fish, disturbed from their environment many leagues under the sea. None of the fishermen had ever seen the likes of what we caught. There were dozens of species all in a bright array of colors, sizes, and shapes. It was frightening to observe that where the depth of the sea, prior to the earthquake, was about 50 fathoms deep it was now 15 fathoms. In other locations, it was reversed. The crushing power of Mother Nature has no boundaries. After a few days, we moved on to Noyes Island in hopes of finding better luck.

I continued fishing with Francis through 1960. My first year with him, I ran the skiff with my partner Jerry Affleck. The next couple of years, I worked as the engineer. Mechanics were not my favorite thing but I struggled through as it was a vital component of maintaining a fishing boat. It was also a "must" if I was going to become a skipper. Engineering duties included greasing hundreds of fittings, lubricating the engine, overseeing the fueling process, and making certain the batteries were always well charged. It taught me to always be vigilant in taking care of equipment. My 1975 Mercedes has nearly 400,000 miles on it and it still drives perfectly.

Despite the challenging and tough work it was always a pleasure working for F.B. I also appreciated his crew who continued to increase my understanding of the behavior of the sea.

In 1961, I was invited to play basketball in the Adirondack Mountains in New York. It would have been my first year not fishing in thirteen years. As it turned out it wasn't meant to be. In late May, the NCAA banned active college players from playing in summer league competition. It had to do with illegal payoffs. So in late May, I called F.B., knowing he probably already had his crew and he did.

I then got a chance (a term meaning a job) with Dominic Svornich on the F/V Scandia. It turned out to be a disaster of a year. I would have ended up owing Dom for my share of the grub and fuel, except prior to the season, Dom's nephew Bob Barcott and I put his net together for a $500.00 fee. I often visited Dom at a nursing home in Anacortes where he resided after a stroke. He died in 2011. The awful season was due to a disastrously poor run and by the very few fishing days allowed by the Alaska Department of Fish and Game (ADF&G).

We had a great crew which was made up of Joe Francin, Don Francin, Don Balthazor, Bob Barcott, and me. We spent a lot time in Juneau and Ketchikan. Joe Francin was very musical and played a great guitar. Bob and I could sing decently so we sang and played at a few bars for food and beer.

After that season we were all dead broke. So before heading back to Santa Clara University for my senior year I worked in Skagit Valley baling hay during the day and at night long shoring at the Port of Anacortes. I have to say that baling hay was the hardest work I have ever done. Long shoring was an interesting experience as well. We had a crew of the same guys that I fished with and we were a hungry bunch. We wanted to make sure we kept our job so we really busted our tail. However, it was a union shop and the other guys were at least 25 years our senior. After about three hours and our doubling the number of cases that the other crews stacked the foreman came over to have a talk. He told us in no uncertain terms to slow down and keep pace with the other crews or we were fired. We were shocked and obviously very naïve. I never forgot that experience when later on I negotiated contracts with various unions. I fully believe in unions and the right to collective bargaining. Yet like so many things in life they often get out of hand and damage all parties.

In November of 1961, while still at Santa Clara, I received a call from Francis Barcott. He asked if I was ready to skipper my own boat. I was absolutely ecstatic. It was a dream of mine from the time I threw my first pair of boots on the Veribus. I was planning on going to law school the following fall and fishing in the summer would correspond perfectly with my plans. Salmon fishing had been a significant part of my life and becoming a skipper was just the next step in a natural progression. So the day after graduation I headed home to Anacortes to accept the helm of the F/V Whitworth, a 1913 wooden, GMAC diesel-powered, Alaska limit seiner. She was in rough shape but I was filled with youthful confidence. I had no idea what was in store for me and my crew.

Over the winter my uncle Tony Francin had prepared (hung) my net. So the crew and I only had to load the net and gear aboard, stash the grub, and fuel up the old girl. The crew included Ron Beirbaum, Joe Blum, Howard and Robert Pearson, Jack Kidder and his 12-year-old son Mike, my cabin boy.

We did have to make one minor alteration to the galley. My cabin was adjacent to the galley and the bunk was only 5' long. It did not by any stretch of the imagination fit my 6'5" frame. So my engineer cut a hole in the wall which separated the galley from my stateroom and built a box about 18" by 18" which allowed me to stretch out. It wasn't pretty, but it worked.

According to my log book, we set sail on June 18, 1962 at 11:03 a.m. Many friends and towns people came down to the dock to see us off. There were the routine tears from sweethearts and mothers.

We were now underway to Southeast Alaska sailing along with the St. Bernadette, Dora R, Marysville and my Captain Farwell's Hansen Handbook. The handbook was written for piloting the inland waters of the Puget Sound, British Columbia and Alaska. It was nearly every skipper's bible. I still have it and keep it in a prominent place on my bookshelf. It is a book full of memories and a few coffee stains.

I remember clearly that departure and my scattered thoughts as we pushed out at the sea, moving sleekly through the Straits of Georgia. It was a perfect

Farewell Anacortes

sun drenched day with azure skies and a slight chop to the sea. I thought back to all the years of dreams, preparation, and hard toil. At that moment, I wouldn't have traded what I was doing for anything. I recorded in the log book that our first night at sea was perfectly clear with a million gems in the sky shining down upon us. I stayed at the helm until daybreak.

Anacortes to Ketchikan was a distance of 575 miles. We followed the same route as when I fished with F.B. Yet every trip was a new adventure and I am continually astonished at the raw beauty of the Inside Passage. The trip takes about 75 hours; we traveled night and day with no scheduled stops.

We arrived at the Union Oil dock in Ketchikan at 11:30 a.m. on June 21st. After we fueled up and took on fresh water we headed north to Icy Straits and Elfin Cove. It rained every day and the sea had a slight chop. We stopped near Point Gardner at an enormous iceberg that was floating off shore. We pulled a pike pole from off the rigging and grabbed the edge of the "berg". A crewman jumped onto the iceberg with an ax and started chopping on the huge piece of ice until several small pieces floated off. We then threw the brailer overboard and scooped up a few chunks. We now had a supply of ice for our icebox. It was great ice as it stayed frozen as a rock for at least 10 days. We were always on the outlook for icebergs both to avoid hitting them and to grab a few chunks for the icebox. The icebergs were spectacular for both their size and for their magnificent blue florescent color. Those floating in Icy Straits broke off from one of the glaciers in the Glacier Bay Basin. Icebergs could be seen floating throughout the region all summer long.

My first year as skipper was demanding. The ugly condition of the boat and equipment subdued the excitement that I anticipated in my first year at the helm. We had engine breakdowns continuously. I was a greenhorn skipper with a boat that was truly a piece of junk. She had been a decent sea boat but there had been virtually no repairs or maintenance done on her for years. The problems were so severe that in retrospect it could have cost us our lives. Today, as I read my log book from 1962 I am still shocked at the adversity we encountered. However, the Lord watched over us.

The most severe problem we had was the condition of the fuel tanks. With the help of Bud, a master mechanic in Wrangell, we installed a series of filters to try and arrest the problem. Bud would never take a dollar from me but when he came aboard we would have a fifth of Seagram's VO on the galley table which he consumed while he worked and there was another bottle for him when he completed the job.

Unfortunately the installations of the filters were to no avail and we resorted to tearing up the deck only to find that the steel tanks completely corroded. There were massive holes on the tops where salt water washed over them. We then resorted to installing 6/100 gallon drums in the fish hold and jury-rigged a copper pipe which ran from the fish hold to the engine. I look back now and believe I must have been half crazy to finish the season with a vessel in that condition. Yet despite these problems we ended up with a decent catch for the season. We caught over 70,000 pink salmon in the Inian Islands and nearly 10,000 sockeye at Noyes Island. Amazingly we were one of the top five producers in our cannery's fleet. I have wondered what we could have produced if we had decent equipment.

Jack Kidder (JD) was my cook for the first two seasons. He was an unadventurous cook who I knew all my life and from the days I fished with FB. He came with me strictly because I agreed to bring his young son Mike along as my cabin boy. J.D. prepared hearty and tasty boat food such as pot roasts, heavy soups and stews. The crew never saw a dessert in J.D.'s galley.

We often went into Juneau on weekends for repairs or for some R&R. We also played a lot of basketball with the local native boys on the cement school courts. The Indian kids were short, but they were great competitors and always gave us a run for it. Basketball was very popular in Alaska as the weather was not conducive to football or baseball.

When in Juneau, we usually tied up at the city dock. There was easy access from the street down the ramp to the boats. One Sunday morning at daybreak, I was lying in my bunk ready to get up when, about 4 feet away, I saw a hand reaching in through the porthole on to a shelf where I kept my binoculars, a Western Bowie knife, my hat, and wallet. I also kept a Colt 45 under my pillow. So I grabbed the pistol and seized the hand and pulled it towards me. The man's steely eyes looked in at me and seeing the pistol jerked his hand away. He dove overboard and began swimming for shore. I ran off a couple of rounds a few fathoms ahead of him just to let him know I didn't welcome his intrusion. I don't think many Alaskan's would have been so sympathetic.

When I first started going to Alaska many men were still wearing side arms in most communities. I thought I was in a cowboy movie.

The last two years I ran the boat, my lifelong friend John Armenia ran our galley. He had been trained by his Aunt Mary, an emigrant who operated a marvelous Italian restaurant in Spokane. John fixed a variety of pasta in tomato-based sauces, veal dishes, and a lot of mashed potatoes and meat dishes. We also had enjoyed T-bone or Porterhouse steaks weekly. The crew appreciated his desserts which were highly prized after a long, hard day. John always made that extra effort throughout his entire life. He also ventured out with meals he hadn't cooked before. They nearly always turned out well and the crew appreciated his creativity and the variety.

One time he bought calves liver. He fixed it up with bacon and onions we all enjoyed it. The catch was that he sort of overbought, thinking that you ate it like a beef roast. He had prepared enough liver for half the fleet and it isn't great as leftovers. John became an outstanding cook and I was still enjoying his cooking up to the time he died in August of 2010. John went on to get his Ph.D. in education and became a school superintendent. He later went on to initiate a graduate program for principals and superintendents at City University in Seattle. John was the consummate educator. He never stopped working for his students, young and old alike. He died at his desk at City University on a Saturday afternoon at 5 p.m. I delivered his eulogy.

I ran the Whitworth for three more years and none were as troubling as that first year. I always was always able to hire a hard-working crew and I felt an enormous responsibility for their safety. Even though I was young I had been trained well and was confident of my skills both in navigation and in purse seining. Yet, at age 22 I realized I didn't have the judgment nor the experience that my peers enjoyed.

One crew member a big burly guy by the name of Joe Blum came up to the bridge as we were just starting to head home to the lower 48. He said that if it were okay with me he wanted to stay in Alaska. He thought it was a fit for him, and he liked the life style. Joe and I attended Santa Clara together where he had majored in biology thinking that he might become a doctor. His decision to stay was a good one. Joe went to work for the Alaska Department of Fish and Game and later became the commissioner. He later moved to Washington State where he took over the reins as fisheries director. He made headlines when he proposed to cut the size of the salmon fleet. It didn't ever happen.

We ran into a few treacherous storms and one major squall that could have turned out to be a disaster. Over the years when I discuss that storm with old crew members the story always gets better. It was late August of 1965 and it had been my poorest season. As we left Ketchikan at the south end of Revillagigedo Channel the wind started gusting. We were headed south to make the last opening of the season near Cape Chacon. As we continued south the wind velocity increased. We were about ten miles from Ketchikan when it began blowing up to 40-45 knots. Our situation was exacerbated by the fact that we had the skiff pulled up on deck, which caused the boat to be less stable especially in a storm.

The wind continued and we searched for the nearest shelter to duck into. As I began the turn towards the bay, the wind was on our port side, and the waves were upwards of fifteen feet. In order to negotiate the heavy seas I had

John Armenia stacking corks

Bringing in the end of the net on the Whitworth

Repairing the brailer

Windy day at Noyes Island

42

Brailing in a load of salmon

Pursing up the bottom of the net

The Skipper directing the skiff

Lifting up the rings

Fred Knapp plunging on the stern

45

Bringing in the net

Mike McGreevy scrubbing the deck

Fred Knapp enjoying the ride

to turn toward the port side every third wave to take the "big" one on the bow. It took us three and a half hours to traverse our way into the protected bay, a mere four miles away.

I was at the wheel on the bridge the entire time, and my hands were so cramped that they wouldn't move. A crewman poured warm water over them until my fingers loosened up and became disengaged from the spokes of the steering wheel.

When we entered the bay, we saw it was full of fishing boats, Coast Guard vessels, U.S. Navy ships, tugs and commercial freighters floating comfortably, waiting out the storm. The obvious question was what had we been doing out there?

John Armenia, our cook, had two chickens roasting in the oven. I was so famished with hunger and the crew was so seasick that, as the story is now told, I inhaled both of those birds. Beside John, the other crewmembers were Fred Knapp, engineer; Bill Sims, deckhand; Lloyd Herman, deckhand; and Hod Pearson, our skiff man. It was a short crew but we all did double duty and at the end of the season there were less shares to divide up. We had one other crewman, interestingly an ex-navy guy, but he became so terrified at Noyes Island that we took him ashore and he went home.

The craziest event in my entire fishing career occurred in late August of 1963. We had moved from the fishing grounds on Noyes Island to Anan Creek, which is northwest of Ketchikan. Anan was known for its huge catches of late-run Pink salmon. We were traveling with F.B. on the St. Bernadette and Les Senff, the skipper of the Dora R. When we arrived, we all went in separate directions, as Anan is a twenty-mile-long narrow inlet.

I headed up towards Windy Bay. It was nearly 100 fathoms deep, and the rocky cliffs at the beach went straight up and down allowing the skiff to nuzzle its nose tightly up against the rocks. As we came around the point into Windy Bay, I saw dozens of fish jumping, all seemingly in the air at the same time. It is said that there are about 1,000 fish in the school for each jumper that you see. I knew immediately that there were sizeable schools of fish just waiting to be caught.

I hollered to Hod to jump in the skiff and to the deck hands to get ready to release the net. I thrusted the throttle to full speed and headed up the beach watching the fathom meter. I had never fished in that location before, but I had carefully checked the charts. The Pinks continued jumping as the tide was ready to start ebbing, which would bring the salmon out of the bay and directly into our nets.

I gave the signal to pull the pelican (the net release), and immediately the skiff was pulling the net off the deck, quickly spinning around and heading to the beach. I directed Hod to snug up against the rocks with my wild hand gyrations. The tide cooperated and as soon as the 250-fathom seine was in the water the three pound Pink salmon were jumping and dancing everywhere in our net. It was a sight to behold. The crew and I were jubilant.

Little did we know that conflict was on its way. Another seiner was headed towards us at break-neck speed. It came right up to our bow. The skipper was yelling, shrieking, and flailing his arms about like a wild man. He claimed that we were fishing in his spot and he wasn't about to allow it. He threw a barrage of expletives the likes of which I had never heard. Of course, there were no proprietary rights to these fishing grounds.

Suddenly, he wheeled around and moved off heading directly into the middle of our net, as his crew threw their anchor overboard. I presumed accurately that he was going to go over our cork line with the intention to rip our net. My urgent concern was for Hod in the skiff, who was still holding the nose of the skiff fast up against the rocks at full throttle.

Unfortunately he was not looking at me for directions (we didn't have walkie talkies or cell phones in those days). If the intruder were to hit the cork line at the speed which he was traveling Hod would have been sent into orbit and that was not going to happen on my watch.

Lloyd Herman was standing next to me on the port side of the bridge and I hollered to him to hand me my rifle, a 360 Magnum Sharpshooter. The rifle was loaded, and I laid three quick rounds about ten or so feet in front of the intruder's bow. He wasn't fazed, and he was getting closer to the cork line by the second. I was a pretty fair shot with a rifle, getting honors in ROTC and shooting rifles since I was a young kid. (My grandmother Augustus Keister first taught me to shoot. She could line up a dozen or so bottles on a fence 100 feet in the distance, and shooting with one arm, knock every one down in seconds. She learned this skill while protecting her family's cattle from wolves in the bitter cold winters of North Dakota.)

My next shot was on their visor, which surrounded his bridge. Apparently he realized that I wasn't kidding, and God help me, I wasn't. A second round followed just as he began wheeling the boat around to head back out of the net. Once again he throttled up to full speed and came back over toward us bumping the midsection of the old Whitworth. And to make things worse, this crazy guy's son was coming at us in his boat. Now we had two madmen yelling and threatening and brandishing their own rifles. We tried ignoring them the best we could and began pulling in our net despite the lunacy.

Then just as we started brailing the fish out of the net (a net laced to a round piece of steel used for unloading the fish) about 7,000 pink salmon aboard, our two allies, the St. Bernadette and Dora R came cruising into the bay. I had never been more thrilled to see anyone. As I was explaining the situation to F.B. and Les, the ruthless guys bolted off.

We were the talk of the fleet for the rest of that season. After the incident it was clear that other boats kept their distance. We unfortunately became known as the insane ones. Years after the confrontation I still tremble to think what could have happened on that fateful day.

The other event that shot tremors down my spine occurred on an evening when we were about to make a set near South Inian Cove in Icy Straits. I gave the signal to release the net when suddenly the leads and rings of the seine got tangled on deck and tumbled off the deck into the sea in one big mess. This huge weight caused the skiff to immediately sink dumping our two skiff men into the icy water. One of those men was my fiancé's kid brother Mike McGreevy. You can imagine what was going through my head. As it mercifully transpired there was no injury except to the skiff. It was under water but remained attached to the end of the net. We easily brought it aboard the Whitworth and headed for Elfin Cove. Fred Knapp, my old friend and our engineer got right to work and in 24 hours we were out fishing again. Fred was our season saver several times that year. He had learned his craft from his father Worth, an old school master mechanic.

Mike McGreevy was this red-headed kid who in later years worked for me in Kodiak. I remember on the weekends him turning the crank on our old ice cream maker. It was the job of the youngest crewman to supply the ice cream. It was a big treat for our crew.

Another event in Anan Creek occurred when we saw a sizable school of fish finning about 50 fathoms out. I threw the throttle in full gear and yelled to the skiff men to get in the skiff. I reached the area where I had seen the school, released the net, and did a round haul on the fish. (A round haul is when the seiner goes around the school of fish without stopping reaching the skiff towing the other end of the net in just minutes.) As we pulled in the net there were odd looking fish gilled in some of the meshes. When we came to the end the net was heavy and to our utter surprise we had a net full of albacore tuna. They were not in great demand by our cannery so we gave away as many as we could to other boats and kept a few for ourselves which John barbequed, baked, and grilled. When I spoke to an Alaska Fish and Game officer he was amazed at our story and I am not sure he even believed me. He had never heard of a school of tuna in Alaska. Yet I knew that the occasional tuna had been caught in Alaskan waters.

One evening in early September of 1965 while heading to Ketchikan we

Aurora Borealis

saw a most astonishing sight. It was the aurora borealis in all its spectacular glory. I had seen the northern lights before but never in such brilliance as that night while approaching Revillagigedo Channel. We shut down the engine and all the crew laid on their backs peering up at the spectacle. There were literally millions of vivid pastel ribbons shooting down upon us like some sort of mysterious weapon. They appeared in the sky as light green, pink, and yellow pinwheels and pillars of light appeared to wave and vibrate. The aurora borealis gets its name from Aurora, the mythical Roman goddess of the dawn and from the Greek name for the north wind, Boreas.

In the northern latitudes the aurora borealis was seen as a symbol of approaching doom and the spectacle was viewed with terror by the Inuit people. One myth relates that the Aurora Borealis is telling stories of what happened in the past and what will happen in the future.

That night we had experienced a very extraordinary ceremony which Mother Nature had orchestrated.

The summer of 1965 was my last year fishing but in my heart I knew I would always be a fisherman.

CHAPTER THREE

MOVING ON

IN NOVEMBER OF 1965 I married Marcia McGreevy. She was from Spokane and we met while I was attending Gonzaga Law School. We raised three children: two boys, John and Matt, and a daughter Megan. Regrettably, the marriage ended in 1983.

In 1966, after graduating from law school, I went to work for a contractor at the Agency for International Development (AID). The job took me to several countries including an extensive stay in Kabul and Kandahar, Afghanistan. I knew so little about foreign affairs.

Afghanistan was a remarkable experience and one I think of often, especially with the horrendous events which have occurred in the first decade of the 21st century.

AID's primary objective was to work with farmers and food processors and to assist them in developing marketable crops for export. It is a fact that the Kandahar Valley, if managed efficiently, could provide a substantial supply of food for the entire region. It was often referred to as the Imperial Valley of the Middle East. I traveled and worked with Matt Looney, our elder statesman and agronomist and Dr. Luis De Alquez, a food scientist.

One morning I was meeting with the manager of a fruit cannery that produced jams, jellies, and juices. As we were talking, Dr. De Alquez came running in screaming about an immense problem he had uncovered. He said that the Afghan company was using formaldehyde as its preservative and it would be fatal to anyone consuming their products. The manager, an Italian national spoke right up and said, "Don't worry, doctor, we ship our entire production to Russia." The doctor was speechless. The rest of us had a good laugh. Little did we realize that in 1979 the Russians would invade Afghanistan. It would come to be known as the "Soviet Union's Vietnam War" it lasted for nine years.

The heat of the summer and fall in Kabul was unbearable, often hitting 110 degrees Fahrenheit. We started work at 4 a.m. so that by noon we took a break at the time when the sun was scorching man, beast and soil alike. We then would start again about 3:00 p.m. The Afghan's preferred to meet in the late afternoon and evening. Often the meetings lasted late into the night.

One late September morning near daybreak I was flying to Kandahar from Kabul in a DC- 3. As I sat in the co-pilot's seat the pilot, an Air Force lieutenant, pointed out what looked to be a pencil line on the desert in the distance. He explained that it was a caravan making its annual trek from the mountains of the Hindu Kush or "Killer of Indians" to Pakistan. The lieutenant said that they were Pathans, the last refuge of nomadic life. The Pathans, at that time, numbered over two million nomads and since time immemorial have been moving their flocks from summer pasturage on the high plateaus of the Hindu Kush to winter quarters on river banks in Pakistan. As we drew nearer, we could see the people and their animals in bands stretching for several miles. It was a coincidence that I was seeing this event, as I had just completed reading James A. Michener's novel Caravans, which I had picked up on a trip to Tokyo.

I found the Afghan men engaging and enjoyable. They were the same in their needs as all other men that I have met throughout our world. They were keen on providing for their families, wanting steady work and to educate their children. Many of the men I met spoke English, as they had worked for American companies such as Bechtel and Morrison Knudsen Corporation which had been there building infrastructure and dams.

I was invited to many of the men's homes for dinner but I was never directly introduced to their wives or daughters. I saw women in the bazaars, but they always wore a burqa or at the least a face veil called a chadri.

I was very impressed at their dedication to ritual prayer, or salat, which they performed five times a day. The Muslim men I worked with would bring to a standstill whatever they were doing, pull out their prayer mat, and face

Mecca to worship Allah. The history of these people is rich and filled with centuries of being tormented by countless warring tribes. And it continues today. Afghanistan is a lost paradise of very remarkable people.

When I would periodically return from Afghanistan I would stop first in Washington. It was to my surprise that Senator Henry Jackson would always know my arrival time and want to visit before I met officially with my boss. I knew there was much more going on in the Middle East than I was aware. I remember reporting to the Senator about an airport and hospital built in Kandahar. Neither had ever been occupied and as I walked through the concourse of the airport there were sand drifts up to my knees. There was no need for the airport since there were no flights coming into the area.

The hospital was of modern construction and ready for occupancy. However, there were no doctors and the equipment stored throughout the facility had never been uncrated. It was the time of the cold war and the philosophy of the state department was to match the Russians dollar for dollar and they had built the airport in Kabul.

In August of 1966, our son John was born, a nine pound healthy boy. I scarcely made it home for his birth, as there were flight complications out of Hong Kong. In spite of the pilot's strike it all worked out. I was told that I was the first father in Spokane ever allowed in the delivery room. I think it was family connections. Our doctor was Jerome Sweeny.

After returning from the Middle East I had a severe stomach disorder. Monthly, I would be terribly ill with a high temperature and miserable cramps. Dr. Sweeny had served in the Naval Battle of Guadalcanal and had observed this illness in that theater. After suffering with this condition for several months I saw Dr. Sweeny who prescribed some medication that I took for a few weeks and the condition never occurred again.

After the Middle East, I went to work for Paul Mariani Jr., the president of Mariani Enterprises in Cupertino, California. I was initially hired as legal counsel however, after only one week on the job Paul fired the president of their frozen food division and asked me to step in as the acting CEO. I enjoyed the challenge and learned how a business really worked. I have always said that I got my law degree from Gonzaga University and my Ph.D. in business from Paul Mariani Jr.

Yet despite the knowledge and experience I was acquiring I was still working for someone and that didn't work for me. I was too independent after those years at sea and running my own ship.

After three years with the Mariani Group, I returned to Seattle to pursue a career in the fish processing business. My first venture was the purchase of a burned-out cannery in Cordova, Alaska. It was formerly the Parks Canning Company, which had been destroyed by a massive fire. The only buildings left were the Filipino bunkhouse, the office, and the cookhouse. My reason for purchasing this burnt out cannery was to acquire its outstanding fleet of gillnet fishermen. Now I could buy the fish but I had no place to process them. So I negotiated a deal with Charlie Alhadoff of the New England Fish Company. We agreed that their plant in Orca, a short distance from Cordova, would custom can our catch for that season. It is interesting to remember that my agreement with Charlie was done with a simple handshake. How things have changed.

The first night I arrived in Cordova to start the season was a hellish nightmare. In those days many of the workers were Filipino. They arrived from Seattle with two bags, one with their work clothes and rain gear and the other filled with half pints of liquor. They had their own bunkhouse and played mahjongg, a rummy type card game, on their time off, which wasn't often during the season. On this particular night there was a hotly contested card game going on with plenty of liquor flowing. There ensued an argument, a pistol was pulled, a shot fired, and a man was dead. It was one hell'uva way to be introduced to Cordova. I quickly learned the deadliness of liquor in the fishing business.

The custom canning agreement worked out well and the next year we built the first plant in Alaska totally devoted to sharp-freezing seafood.

On the Copper River in those days the processors gave the fishermen poker like chips on the fishing grounds when they delivered their fish to the tender. Then at the end of the season, they turned them in for cash. At that time, the fish were still bought by the piece so there was no need to weigh them. There was a red chip for Sockeye, blue for Coho's, and white for Kings.

When the season ended we hung a sign on our office door announcing the hours when the pay clerk would be available to settle accounts. It wasn't just a simple calculation as there were always advances made for fuel, grub, repairs, and checks sent home to family. Often the canneries funded the fishermen during the winter as well as in the years when the fishing was dismal. I understood from my staff that the fishermen would line up in the morning and the settlements were completed by noon. On payday the clerk came to me and explained that he still had 30 percent of the cash remaining. I was walking back to his office just as Miss Emilie, the local madam arrived in her fringed skirts, holding up her parasol and carrying a large knitting bag. She marched up to the counter, dumped out her chips, and said, "Okay boys, let's see the green." I will never forget that day as long as I live. Miss Emilie was the "high liner" of our fleet and never would cast a net.

I got to know Miss Emilie and enjoyed her lusty and licentious stories of the many singers and sinners she knew or employed. She related many gold rush stories and explained that women burned with the gold fever just as much as the men. She said she was no exception. I have to say she had pluck and great business savvy. She was also an awesome cook who taught me how to grill razor clams that were absolutely scrumptious.

I shortly sold my interest in the Cordova plant to Bob Morgan who was the nephew of Harold Parks, the founder and owner of the former Parks Canning Company.

In early 1969, I also entered into a partnership with a fellow alumnus of Santa Clara University, Jerry Williamson. We formed Europe Pacific International Corporation (EPIC). However, the most significant event of 1969 was the birth of our second son, Matthew McGreevy Keister.

In 1971, EPIC purchased from Harry Felton Middle Bay Fisheries, a processing plant in Kodiak. Harry a Montanan turned Alaskan was dying of cancer. I made the deal to buy his plant in a Missoula hospital. Harry was a guy's guy and died way too early from that dreaded disease. I remember the outstanding seafood dinners at his home in Kodiak prepared by Lorraine his flaming red-haired wife.

After one year of operation, I ended up buying Middle Bay Fisheries from

EPIC. Jerry had no stomach for the high-risk fish processing business. He was strictly a marketing guy. In the same year I purchased American Cold Storage, a cold storage warehouse and ice plant in Everett, Washington. The cold storage warehouse became pivotal to our seafood operations. We did all of our distribution from that location along with packaging and re-packing of product into consumer-size units. It was also the accounting and administrative offices for my Alaska and Canadian operations. It also provided work for many of our seasonal workers from Alaska.

One of the pivotal men on our management team was Gordon Heitman. Gordon was seventy-five years of age when he started working for me in 1972 as our chief financial officer. He had a world of experience which he gained riding the rails auditing wallpaper plants for Sears, Roebuck & Company. We often drove to Vancouver, B.C., leaving early in the morning and returning late in the afternoon. He had countless stories and they nearly always had a salient business point to them. Those were long days and on the return trip home Gordon would insert a classical eight-track cartridge into the stereo and promptly fall asleep.

Our Canadian operation specialized in preparing lox for the New York & Toronto Jewish market. Lox are a delicately cured smoked salmon. The West Coast of Vancouver Island, near Tofino, produced the best King salmon in the world and their abundant size made them just right for preparing lox. These enormous Kings were handled and frozen with utmost care. Each afternoon the specialists would take 10 or 12 of these exceptional fish from the freezer to thaw. When they arrived at work the next morning at 4:00 a.m. the fish were ready to be prepared. It was remarkable to watch these artists perform their skills on these prized fish.

Gordon was still working for me when he reached ninety years of age. His eyesight was failing so three days a week I would send a car to his home and bring him to the Everett office. His health was waning and his appearance at the office became less frequent. In the summer of 1988 I received a call from his daughter. Gordon's health was worsening and she didn't expect him to live through the night. I booked a flight from Anchorage and arrived at the hospital in Seattle a few hours later. His nurse told me that he had been in and out of consciousness for the past several days. As I walked into his room he was motionless. I sat down next to him and grasped his timeworn hand. After a few minutes he turned over to me and inquired, "How's fishing?" and lay back down. Several minutes later he lifted his hand, pointed his thumb skyward, and said, "I'll see you up there." Those were his last words; he died minutes later.

Middle Bay Fisheries was located on the northeast side of Kodiak Island in a secluded area. Each April Bob Barcott and I would snow shoe into the plant with packs on our back to start preparing the plant ready for the season. The first thing we did was to launch the dory and to sail nearby setting out a few King crab pots. We feasted on the local seafood delicacies for several days until we managed to get a truck operational for a trip to the grocery store in Kodiak. It was about a twenty-mile drive on the shoddiest road you can imagine.

It was always a challenge to get workers out to this remote plant. After our first year we recruited students from Santa Clara University and their friends. This was a strategy we continued to employ for many years.

During the period throngs of hippies lived in the surrounding woods. My son John, who was age five would see smoke in the woods and say, "Hey Dad, look and see the hippies."

A few years later, son Matt would travel to Kodiak with me. After an early breakfast he would go out on the dock and fish until noon have lunch and go back out fishing until dark. He loved to fish even though the only thing he caught was ratfish and other scavengers. However, he caught a lot of them and that was all that counted.

In all my wisdom I thought I would revolutionize the fish processing business. So one winter I visited several chicken-slaughtering plants in Georgia. There I saw a steel device that circled the butchering area and on elongated hooks the workers attached the chickens. As it circled around each person had a specific butchering job. I bought one of the damned things and shipped it to our Kodiak plant where my engineers installed it. When my crew of Native Americans and Eskimos saw the apparatus they voiced grave doubts about it and my sanity. They thought I was plum crazy. We did finally get it to operate but it was not nearly the labor savings device I had imagined.

Middle Bay was built to process salmon but King crab became our main product. Those were the heyday years when King crab was literally the "King". The crab boats would come to our dock loaded to the scuppers and the price often exceeded a $1.00 per pound. This was an enormous price compared to the price paid for other species of fish in the 1970's. The average boat grossed about a million dollars each season. In those times the city of Kodiak was a colorful and lively place. All of the things that you would read about in the gold rush days also occurred in Kodiak. There was illegal gambling, con-man schemes, and rampant prostitution.

I had a friend in San Francisco whose son worked for us one season. He fell "in love" with a go-go dancer at Mike's Place, a local strip joint. He brought the girl out to the plant and proposed to her on our dock. It was a typical bitter cold and blustery day. He gave her a full carat diamond ring and off she went back to town for work. He never saw her again.

Whenever I would arrive at Middle Bay, our head floor lady would always have prepared for me a container of King crab merus legs. It was all I ate from the time I arrived until I departed. The merus is the most prized flank of crabmeat that is extracted from the largest section in each King crab leg. We processed huge quantities of King crab into meat. After the extraction from the shell the meat was placed in metal containers called long boys which were frozen into 30 pound blocks. They were like gold.

One December just before Christmas, we shipped a full truckload of these blocks of crabmeat to New York City to a reputable seafood purveyor. When the truck driver drove down the dark alley to the customer's warehouse he was directed by "someone" to unload just a short distance down the alley. The driver followed the instructions and on Monday morning our customer called looking for his shipment. The trucking company's insurance paid us. It was a full load (40,000 pounds) at @$20 per pound.

In 1976, I bought Reliance Fish Company, a venerable Vancouver, B.C. fish processing and distribution company from an established Icelandic family. Shortly thereafter we received a letter from the B.C. Provincial Government stating that since the new owners were "foreigners" the company would not be able to service the government contracts, which represented nearly 50 percent of the company's revenue. Reliance was a processor, but it also was a major distributor of seafood throughout British Columbia and the Prairie Provinces. The majority of Reliance's business was providing the military, the parks, and other government agencies with enormous amounts of seafood. So I was forced to sell and the only candidate that I could find who was financially elgible was Dan Lee. Dan was a feisty, pint-sized man of Chinese descent, but a full-sized man of virtue and business acumen. He had immigrated to Canada as a young man and became a successful businessman. He gave me a fair price and it turned out to be a win-win situation. We stayed friends for another decade and whenever I was in Vancouver he treated me to a splendid Chinese dinner.

In 1978 I sold the Middle Bay plant. The King crab was nearly fished out. It was the same story that had occurred for decades before with all the other species of fish. It continues today with nearly every species of harvestable seafood in all the fishing banks around the world being depleted by corporate greed. Overfishing has exhausted fish populations to the point where large-scale commercial fishing around the world is no longer economically viable.

During this time I partnered with Alvah Hales, an ambitious man from Florida with an eighth grade formal education but tremendous shrewdness. Our goal was to purchase the Japanese processing vessel, the Shinana Maru. It was for sale and had been slated to be shipped to Korea for scrapping. It had been the world's largest seafood processing vessel and was nearly a thousand feet in length and capable of both canning and freezing. It was our idea to refurbish this colossal vessel and to operate it in Alaska. We had arranged the financing and I traveled to Tokyo to consummate the purchase. I then arranged for the ship to be towed to Shanghai where we intended to do the refurbishing.

It was 1972, the year President Nixon and Secretary of State Kissinger completed a new treaty with China, which reestablished normal relations with the People's Republic of China. American citizens were once again allowed to travel to China and we were among the first U.S. citizens to do so. Upon my arrival I was taken to a grand old hotel that hadn't been occupied for nearly 30 years. When we were taken to our rooms the furniture was still covered with white yellow-stained sheets, and the dust had not yet been vacuumed.

In my suite of rooms an army soldier with a weapon was posted at the entrance to the kitchen and another right outside the door. Our negotiations were held in the great room of the suite where a table for sixteen was prepared. I was not allowed to leave the hotel without an escort, but I was permitted to go to the park across the street to participate in a Tai Chi class.

The small restaurant in the hotel had very few western dishes and I remember eating hard boiled eggs, toast, and coffee several mornings. It was a far cry from the luxurious hotels found in China today.

There were numerous government representatives at all our meetings and they appeared totally skeptical of each other. They all wanted a piece of the proposed business for their respective government section. They individually and collectively lacked negotiating skills and possessed even less tact. We struggled with this negotiation for a week at which time we threw in the towel. The vessel was never refurbished and we sold it shortly thereafter.

Alvah died of a massive heart attack near his home in Ronald, Washington while chopping wood. He was in his mid-forties.

For the next two years my company only processed fish in British Columbia, Oregon, and Washington. All products were hauled to the Everett plant, where it was either sold fresh or frozen.

In the spring of 1979, we had a major herring roe fisheries in British Columbia. On the Thursday before Easter, Del Molenkamp, our operations manager called in from the fishing grounds north of Nanaimo. He stated that most of the B.C. fish packers had taken off for the Easter weekend and that we would have a singular opportunity to grab a big share of the herring since the run was nearing its peak. I agreed with him and sent Mary Curry with her knitting bags filled with cash to rendezvous with him. It was imperative that he have the cash as the Canadian boats sold only for cash to us Yankees. Del was right on and the big run hit that weekend filling all our tenders with ripe, mature herring. Kazunoko, as it is called in Japan, is particularly prized in the Japanese market on their New Year.

In 1980 I purchased the Alaska Salmon Company taking over their plant on East 70th Street in Anchorage. We also leased another plant from the state on the other side of town. I was now back in the Alaska fisheries in a major way. These were wild years as fish prices were high and the market for Alaskan salmon in Japan was at its peak. We processed millions of pounds of salmon each year from 1980 through 1988.

During this period I made numerous business trips to the Far East including Japan, Korea, Hong Kong, China, Thailand, and Taipei. They were marvelous adventures and of course a lot of stories resulted.

One trip to Japan that I will never forget occurred after I had negotiated a contract with Daiei, a major chain store. According to the custom I flew to Tokyo to celebrate our successful new business relationship. Several of the corporate chiefs greeted me at my hotel. They informed me that we were going to a party. So off we went in a formation of limousines, seven officers and directors of Daiei and me.

It was my first Japanese event hosted by geishas. As we sat down at the Tribeca-style rectangular table, I saw that a geisha was seated between each man. In front of each geisha was placed a bottle of Scotch whiskey, a bottle of Japanese beer, and a ceramic flask of sake. The food soon arrived and as each man took a drink from any one of the three glasses in front of him a geisha immediately refilled his glass. It didn't take long to see where this was going.

Dinner proceeded and the geishas played their traditional string instruments and performed elegant and graceful dances. A geisha is a traditional Japanese entertainer not to be mistaken for a courtesan. As the night wore on the Japanese men, most of whom have very good singing voices, got up and sang a song or two. After a while they were insistent that I sing too. I made excuses and thought they would soon be too drunk to be concerned. Not the case, they continued to pursue me. Finally I simply said that I never sing without a band. In their drunkenness they appeared to accept that explanation, however, I saw lot of talking going on. Sure enough, in about thirty minutes, a five-piece band arrived and I had no choice but to sing and I chose the Irish ballad "Danny Boy." By the time I sung I don't think many of my hosts were still standing. I am still always amused when I hear that old song playing.

One gray October day, I received a letter from a Japanese trading company with which we did a substantial amount of business. They were making a claim as to the quality of the fish they had received. It was a substantial quantity, seven containers of chum salmon. They claimed the fish were water-marked and not in compliance with the sample they had received and approved. Seven containers amounted to about 280,000 pounds. It was a major claim. I booked a flight and went off to Sapporo, the largest city on the island of Hokkaido. Hokkaido is the northernmost island of the 47 prefectural-level subdivisions of Japan. The morning of my arrival, a group of representatives from the company accompanied me to their customer's warehouse. They had prepared a cold room where samples of the product were laid out for inspection. I viewed the samples thoroughly and was skeptical that they were fish that we had shipped. However, I had no clear evidence. I then asked that a dozen full cases be brought out for my review. Soon a forklift delivered them out. Immediately I noticed that the steel strapping material on the 100-pound fiber boxes was not what I thought our plant used. I continued the inspection, and when I returned to the hotel I called the superintendent of our plant where the product was packaged. He confirmed that the strapping material that we used was a blue synthetic material.

I then requested that three of the boxes that I had inspected be air shipped back to the states. I politely said that they would receive a prompt reply to their claim and departed for the airport. When the three cases arrived our quality control manager sent samples of the fish scales to a fisheries laboratory for testing. It was immediately determined that the fish had not been caught in Alaska waters but were of Russian origin. There was a fish-switch, and therefore the claim was wrongful.

In every Asian country I visited my hosts were cordial and accepting of my Western ways. I learned enough words in each language to greet people properly and to know enough words to order food, get my needs met at hotels, and to be able to have a taxi driver return me to my hotel. I found the cuisine of the Far East intriguing and being adventurous I tried all kinds of foods, many of which I was not sure what I was eating.

When my son Matt was fourteen he joined me on a trip to Guangzhou, China, where we were buying white shrimp. This was a time when China was first becoming free of their ties to the Communist economic theory. It was an extraordinary time to be in China. One day we were invited to take a field trip to a small seaside town where we were shown shrimp that they were harvesting. After the viewing we went to a small inn where lunch was being served. I was seated at the guest table and Matt was seated with the Minister of Propaganda, a few tables in front of me. The minister was very thoughtful to Matt and he fortunately spoke some English. Our first course was boiling hot broth served in legendary porcelain bowls. Just as I was about to spoon the liquid into my mouth a server came by pouring tiny live creatures into the mixture. I carefully looked to see how Matt was doing and to my astonishment the minister had him fully engaged and Matt was taking it all in stride. I learned later these tiny creatures were baby snakes.

In 1985, I purchased the legendary Wakefield processing plant in Seldovia from the Sea Galley Restaurant chain. Wakefield Fisheries was a pioneer in King crab production and had developed many of the processing techniques that made the crab industry commercially viable. The area surrounding Seldovia is a celebration of rugged snow-capped mountains, glaciers that stretch from the sea for miles and incredible icy blue water. There may have been more emotion involved in buying that plant than good business judgment.

Seldovia became our flagship plant and all of our team was proud of this facility. Seldovia was a picturesque village founded by the Russians around 1844 for its abundant fur and fish resources, especially herring. In fact the word "Seldovia", translates as herring in the Russian language. In early years Seldovia was inhabited by Eskimos, Aleuts, and Dena'ina Indians, who had come there for its rich resources.

The Seldovia facility was known as the Wakefield Plant and was once owned by Lowell Wakefield who had lived in Anacortes in a lovely home near the high school. It was later purchased by the Maynard Lewis family. Coincidentally in 1988, Maynard's three daughters, grandson, and granddaughter all worked at our Seldovia plant.

We had a solid crew in Seldovia including Dick Schamp, Keith Robbins, and Rick Newell. However, Seldovia was always kind of a mystery. Things went on in Seldovia that I was not aware of. We had workers, mainly college kids, who came from nearly every state. They loved the area and the relationships that they developed. They were treated well. We built a very comfortable bunkhouse for the crew and the galley was open 24 hours a day. The work was tough, wet, and cold. When the fish arrived we worked until every last fish was processed, often 16 to 18 hour shifts. And when things were slow the crew slept until the next silver hoarde arrived.

My favorite time during that era was flying from Anchorage to Seldovia on Friday afternoons just in time to watch the fleet of gillnetters and purse seiners begin pulling into our dock to sell their day's catch of salmon.

I remember gazing out and seeing dozens of tiny specks on the bright orange horizon as the midnight sun began its nightly ritual. The specks became larger and larger until I could see the vessels barreling at full speed to reach the dock.

On Sundays, our assistant plant manager's wife fixed a sumptuous dinner of local seafood for our management crew. I especially remember the King crab enchiladas that she prepared. Unfortunately she had other things going on including selling pot. One night she borrowed the company truck and made "a delivery" out in Jakolof Bay. The authorities snagged her and our truck. After a few months we got the truck back, but she did a short stint in the pokey.

One Sunday a few of the crew and I took a jeep up into the nearby mountains to pick blueberries. I was out about 30 yards or so picking away and facing the jeep. Suddenly I felt a breeze blow by me and heard a sudden crash. A black bear was about to take a swipe at me when the same lady mentioned above with her side arm put a bullet in that bear right between its eyes. It was a perfect shot. It was a good thing, as that bear was big enough to do some serious injury. I am always amazed at how quietly a creature of that size can creep around in its environs.

I had many loyal employees but none more devoted than Dan McGreevy. Dan was in charge of our quality control department. He was the best and our product was prized in the worldwide seafood market because of his intelligent and laborious work.

Dan did other duties that didn't have to do with the quality control. One season we had an Italian mafia-type named Angelo buying fish for us in lower

Cook Inlet. Our management had agreed to advance him $100,000 for his fish-buying fund and Dan was to deliver the cash. He drove down to Homer, a village at the southern tip of the Kenai Peninsula. As the story goes, Dan met Angelo in a restaurant and as Dan sat down he placed his .357magnum pistol on the table. He then pulled out the cash telling Angelo in no uncertain terms that if every damned dollar wasn't accounted for that he would personally pay him a very unpleasant visit. Angelo's accounting turned out to be impeccable. And he hustled a whole bunch of fish as well.

One Friday afternoon in mid-July of 1986, Delmar Molenkamp, my most loyal confidant, asked for $150,000 in cash to be flown out to him in King Salmon, where our Bristol Bay buying station was located. He needed it for a weekend Sockeye opening, predicted to be the peak of the run. Roy Jones, our senior operation man in Anchorage, went to the bank and got the cash. It was not unusual for the banks to have large quantities of cash available for fish-buying purposes. As standard procedure the cash was packed in 6" x 12" x 16" wooden caviar boxes and nailed tightly down. Roy then ran the boxes out to the freight airport and shipped them out on Wien Airlines. When the cache arrived in King Salmon, the freight clerk, thinking something was awry, called the Alaska State Troopers. Despite Delmar's protest, the trooper opened up the boxes finding the cash. Del explained the situation but the trooper didn't buy it and decided to let the judge make the decision and he seized the money. Unfortunately we couldn't arrange a hearing until Monday losing the opportunity to buy fish over the weekend. The judge released the money after Del related the facts and he confirmed with our bank that the cash was legal.

In 1987 my longtime friend and college roommate, Barry Cristina and his dad Vernon visited me in Alaska. I gave them a whirlwind tour of our facilities in Anchorage, Bristol Bay, and Seldovia.

One morning we departed King Salmon in our Cessna 360 heading to Seldovia. My most experienced bush pilot was at the controls. We cruised along the Naknek River until unexpectedly we hit a solid fog bank. The pilot instantly pulled back hard on the yoke placing the aircraft in a near vertical position. Vernon went wild screaming at the pilot to put the dammed plane down and do it at this instant. The pilot looked sympathetically at Vernon who was sitting beside him in the co-pilot's seat. He calmly said we would be out of the fog in just a moment and before the words were out of his mouth we were. As we started over the mountain range I looked out our starboard side and there was a Cessna 180 that had crashed a few days earlier lying in a crevice. Thankfully, Vernon didn't see it.

My daughter Megan who was 13 years old traveled with us. She was seated in the stern in the jump seat. I remember her yelling out, "Daddy my tummy hurts" and I am sure it did. She was a real trooper and my lovely traveling companion for many summers. We traveled throughout Central and South-central Alaska visiting our plants, fishermen and buying stations. Due to the weather we were often stranded in a desolate village with very humble or no accommodations.

In the spring, I often would drive a new vehicle from Seattle to our plant in Anchorage. One year Megan and her friend Amber accompanied me. They were fourteen years of age and big into music. They had brought with them several cassettes of Whitney Houston's music that they played continually on our seven-day trip. It was great fun showing the girls the interior of British Columbia and Alaska. Yet after that trip I was no longer a big fan of Whitney Houston.

CHAPTER FOUR

It Was Over

~~~~~~

ALL OF THESE STORIES are humbled by my final episode in the fishing industry. In the early morning of March 24, 1989 I was returning by air to Seattle from Anchorage. On the flight I learned that heavy crude oil was leaking from the tanker Exxon Valdez, which had hit Bligh Reef in Prince William Sound. The giant supertanker had gutted her hull spilling some 30 million gallons of crude oil into the water. When I landed in Seattle I called my Anchorage office and received only scanty details.

I booked the next flight, and four hours later I was back in Anchorage. A charter plane had been arranged, and off I went to try and determine the extent of the spill. When we approached the crippled vessel lying helpless and still on the rocks I became ill, shaken to the bone. Oil was blanketing the Sound and its beaches. We flew west following the stream of oil which had already moved several miles. There was no doubt this was going to be a disaster of untold proportions. I felt anger beyond what I had ever experienced. I could not comprehend 30,000,000 gallons of crude oil in the pristine Prince William Sound.

Then after a few days of calm weather a fierce storm blew the oil out into the Gulf of Alaska towards Kodiak and ultimately west to the Alaska Peninsula some 1,500 miles from where the spill occurred.

As expected the Alaska Department of Fish and Game Department closed all of the waters for fishing in and around the Prince William Sound area. Sadly the spill coincided with the herring roe season the most lucrative fishing

69

season for both fishermen and processors.

The next several weeks we spent filing claims and trying to figure out a means by which to maintain our staff and personnel. Each day we would wait for news from Fish and Game. However, the closures continued as the oil drifted farther west and more areas became contaminated.

Communities attempted to block the oil from intruding on their shores by setting up a variety of creative barricades. Nothing proved effective. Moreover, the oil nodules would move about with the tide and rolled up like snowballs. When they reached the size of a basketball they sank to the bottom. Many of the fish such as gray cod, black cod, crab, halibut and other bottom feeding fish consumed and ingested these deadly, black oil balls.

As it happens that winter we had built two 250,000 gallon stainless steel tanks for storing live King and Dungeness crab at our Seldovia plant. King crab was a major production for us and during the season we would ship live crab to Tokyo several times a week. We packed each crab in wet newspaper, placed them in a 100-pound wet lock box and added frozen ice packs. We then loaded them aboard a small plane which took them to Anchorage where they were packed into a 747 headed to Japan. The live crab was a delicacy in the exclusive restaurants of Tokyo and other major cities in Japan, which charged over $100 U.S. per pound.

We never envisaged that we would christen our new live tanks as a shelter for oiled otter, seal, and hundreds of sea-birds including cormorants, ducks, murres, marbled murrelets, gulls, and a myriad of petrels. Dozens of volunteers came from all over the country to assist in the recovery. The volunteers attempted to clean the oiled and frightened creatures. Yet despite their heroic efforts as soon as the birds were released they returned to the beaches only to become oiled once again. It was a morbid situation.

A similar sickening incident struck in April of 2010 when the Deepwater Horizon oil spill (BP Spill) occurred in the Gulf of Mexico. It was astonishing to me what minimal improvements had been made in oil recovery methods. I heard the same questions and concerns from fisherman and business men in the Gulf that I listen to 21 years earlier in Alaska.

The Exxon claims office was initially in Cordova and for several weeks I would fly to Cordova with papers, affidavits, and bills to meet with Exxon representatives. The city was so overcrowded with claimants that at least one time I slept in a sleeping bag in someone's garage who charged me a $100 bucks a night.

The money that flowed during the cleanup period was marked with greed; it was every man for himself. Initially the Exxon staff was cordial and even helpful and I thought for a time that the whole claims process would be handled fairly and ethically. However, as the weeks went by the process became more challenging and the Exxon officials more problematical.

Despite the odds we struggled through the 1990 and 1991 seasons burning through capital. The Pink salmon that returned in 1990 were midgets. The average size was usually 2½ to 3 pounds. What we harvested that year averaged less than 1 pound. There was no market for these fish. We attempted to haul fish in from other fishing areas, but it was tough to break into a new region that was already being served by other producers. There was also the added cost of transporting from distant areas. Alaska is no small territory. In 1991, we negotiated a cost-plus contract with a Seattle-based marketing company. However, due to a myriad of circumstances they defaulted. It was the final whistle.

In June of 2002, after struggling for nearly 14 years with the damage process, I threw in the towel with my Exxon claim. The legal fees were exorbitant and the law firm I had engaged was demanding another $100,000 to continue.

Finally, in 2008, the U.S Supreme Court agreed to hear Exxon's appeal. I knew in my gut that it was over. And on June 25, 2008, the Court found for Exxon. It was just nine months short of twenty years since that chilling disaster on Bligh Reef. I don't think the verdict surprised anyone. Big oil is king, always was and most likely always will be. The bottom line is that the laws designed to prevent and respond to oil spills do not work to protect the public interest when powerful corporations such as Exxon spill oil.

However, in response to the outrage of the public, the U.S. Congress passed the Oil Pollution Act of 1990. The main goal of OPA was to improve the nation's ability to prevent and respond to oil spills. At the time of this printing nearly 86 percent of oil-carrying barges that operate in U.S. waters are doubled hulled.

I still miss the fishing business and especially the fishermen. Every spring I get that longing to head back to Alaska. I am certain that will never change, after all I spent over thirty-five years in the vast and magnificent 49th state.

Salmon Seiner

Flood tide pulling
strong and hard,
nets heavy.
Early gold-sun shadows glisten,
off scraggly Sitka Cypress.
Crew up before dawn,
defying bone-chilling glacier winds
blowing through layers,
of wool and rubber.

The icy, black sea
reveals no trace of life
as crewmen pull ferociously
on strained hemp lines,
their boat heaving
and groaning.

The crew tugs at the web,
as it rolls over the steely
Puretic power block
swinging precariously
from atop the boom.

A tall lanky kid balances
gracefully on the edge
of the turntable
meticulously stacking Spanish corks,
in perfect symmetrical rows.

Out fifty fathoms,
a Sockeye jumps along the cork line,
as others fin in the center of the seine.
The pace quickens and emotions build.
A silvery salmon emerges,
gilled in a mesh,
and another and another.
The tension mounts.

As the end of the seine
is dragged aboard,
all hands rush to the bulwarks.
There are thousands,
a silver horde
of the finest
blood red Sockeye.

Sebastian-Stuart Fish Company

See over there
near the West side,
the cannery,
weather beaten and broken now.
No longer the bright wet-red color
that distinguished salmon canneries
from Astoria to Blaine from Ketchikan
to Cordova and Seldovia to Bristol Bay.
And there beyond the battered piles
was grandpa's musky smelling net shed
It's hidden behind that rusty chicken wire.

Oh, those sunny late spring days
racing breathlessly down that dusty
gravel road to the cannery
where there was wonderful commotion
as fishermen, tender men, cannery me, dockworkers
and day laborers were all caught up in the frenzy.

It was "get ready" time for the salmon season
and there was goings on everywhere.
Freshly painted yellow fork lifts
steaming about unloading enormous trucks
delivering tin cans and cartons.
Mechanics in oily overalls overhauling
touchy seamers, while technicians
from out-of-town in olive drab outfits
tested the aluminum coated, coffin like cookers
with manifold gauges as men in black hats
and black ties watched and smoked.

Oh how the excitement grew,
as the old shed was cracked open,
where the mysteries of the wily salmon
were stored over the long winter months.
The cavernous tomb filled to capacity
with hay-colored, manila purse lines
meticulously coiled in sky high piles
while worn Spanish corks on mile long
lines were strung from the rafters.
On the wooden deck half pound
silver leads stacked in sturdy wooden kegs
waited to be sewn onto kinky
half-inch lines, still incased
in thick coarse and oily burlap sacks.
The cotton web stored
under tons of coarse rock salt
preserving it over the winter
from decay.

The old Sebastian-Stuart Fish Company in Anacortes

A Tale Untold

A SHORT STORY

SELDOVIA WAS ALWAYS A FISHING VILLAGE, at least, as far back as anyone could remember. Everyone who lived there was touched by the wile, Silver salmon. Then back in '64, a great earthquake erupted. It destroyed much of the village and all of the fish canneries. Only one cannery rebuilt, which remained the sole artery to the old ways.

Winters in Seldovia were protracted and bitter cold. Yet, when spring arrived and the ice cracked on the lake by old' Sven's cabin, winter was quickly forgotten. In mid-April the first freighter of the year would call. It unloaded an assortment of supplies including outboard engines, nets, paint, plywood, groceries and an abundance of beer and liquor.

Once the supplies had arrived, the villagers started their preparations for the salmon season. The fishermen and local craftsmen repaired engines, caulked hulls, painted and everything else required to get the boats outfitted for the season. Meanwhile the experienced crewmen were assigned to mending and building nets. The village was abuzz with its people talking of the upcoming season, the boundless salmon runs of the past, and the highline skippers who would make the record-breaking catches.

In early May the cannery hired its crew and the perpetually scarce money started being exchanged. It was distributed in the form of payroll and advances. The advances were made to reliable skippers for their coming season's catch, many of whom never got out of debt to the canneries. The fresh money flowed to the general store to be applied on delinquent accounts, to the fuel dock, and to the cafes and bars. Sullen winter dispositions suddenly turned to smiles and friendliness.

Dan grew up in Northern Montana where his folks owned a cattle ranch. Long days, hard work and severe winters were a part of his youth. After he returned from Vietnam, where he served in the army, he headed for Alaska. He worked his way north aboard an old, Alaska Steamship freighter, by chipping paint in return for passage. When the steaming vessel arrived in Seldovia, it moved slowly into the harbor, just as dawn had broken. When Dan heard the engines slowing down, he rushed from his bunk to the deck, the chilly salt air quickly awakened him. All his life he dreamed of the 49th state and read everything he could get his hands on. Yet, even in his wildest feelings, he never imagined that it could be so awe-inspiring. Straightaway he realized that Seldovia was going to be home.

Seldovia lay hidden near the entrance to Cook Inlet, hugging the coastline just inside Seldovia Bay. An ancient boardwalk which framed the unique village, like a prized work of art, surrounded it. Each day, on the flood tide, huge surges of water from Cook Inlet created tidal changes of over thirty feet. While high above lofty, snow laden mountains protected the village like mystical gods. A spiritual emotion grabbed at Dan, nothing he could really explain, but nothing he could escape from either.

Dan got a job his first summer with an old timer who ran an even older purse seiner. Ben Jack had a drinking problem and often didn't make it out of port in time for an opening. Dan learned a lot from old Ben and his crew. Occasionally he was given the opportunity to take the helm. Ben was an outstanding skipper when he was sober. Dan learned that alcohol was a major problem in the fish business. The following winter was rough for Dan. If he hadn't killed a moose in the fall he never would have been able to stay the winter. Now with spring approaching he was nearly flat broke, like most of the locals.

The past summer's salmon season was disastrous, fish prices had been at a record low and the catches were meager. Then, to make things even sorrier, the Alaska Department of Fish and Game, which regulated fishing, determined not to open the winter King crab season. The test catches indicated only a minimal number of harvestable crab in the Inlet. It was an age-old story, too much over fishing, for too many years, for too little crab.

Now his first winter was over and he'd survived. He knew he could get a decking job on a better boat but decided to sail with Ben again. He wasn't really certain of his reasons but his intuition told him that it would be the soundest decision. The second and the third season were considerably better than that first year and he grossed enough to have a couple of half decent winters. Yet, most importantly he learned an enormous amount; Ben and his crew instructed him about tides, currents and how to properly hang a seine net. He enjoyed learning everything he could.

After surviving a third winter, Dan experienced the spring fever of the upcoming season. Rumors had it that his old skipper Ben Jack, was terribly ill and that most likely would not be fishing any longer. He had crewed for Ben all three seasons that he was in Seldovia aboard the Gull Wing, a cranky but reliable old boat. He knew her from top to bottom. Dan decided he would approach Ivan, the cannery superintendent, about skippering the Gull Wing. The cannery owned her, like they did most of the purse seiners in the fleet. Dan had no doubt about his ability to handle her. He headed down to the boat harbor where the Gull Wing was moored to see how she had weathered the winter.

That night Dan visualized skippering the Gull Wing. In the morning he got up at 5:00 a.m., put on the coffee pot and sat down on the edge of his bed. He peered out into the lazy lagoon where smoky patches of fog shrouded the far bank. Dan had a great affection for the view from his ancient, Russian cabin. The three-room structure, built on the old boardwalk was unpretentious but it was adequate for him and he owned it free and clear. He drank a couple cups of coffee and his stomach growled. He realized that he hadn't eaten since noon the previous day. His mind had been solely focused on the Gull Wing. Hurriedly, he got dressed and headed down to the Harbor Cafe.

As Dan walked down the old boardwalk, he wondered if Ivan would give him the opportunity. "Why wouldn't he?" Dan asked himself. The cannery boss knew he had worked for one of the best fishermen in the village. He had even skippered the Gull Wing for three weeks, when Ben made an emergency trip to Seattle. Dan's mind raced, as he questioned how he could convince Ivan of his capability. When he passed the white-planked Russian Orthodox Church he said a quick prayer. He hastened his pace, as the wind gusted a stiff thirty knots. As he approached the dreary yellow and white cafe an icy chill ran through his bones. He opened the door, walked in and sat down at the counter.

"Morning Slim." Dan said

"What can I get you?" Slim asked.

"Ham and eggs."

"You got it. You can pour your own coffee," Slim called out, as he walked to the grill.

Dan went to the coffee pot just as the door opened and Ivan walked in. He was the same height as Dan, but had a belly, which hung over his "Frisco" jeans. His reddish colored beard was untrimmed.

"Hello Dan, good morning Slim, fix me the usual." Ivan barked out.

"Morning Ivan," Dan replied, "I was coming down to see you."

"Well come on over and join me, it will save you a trip. It's damn cold out there."

Ivan poured himself a mug of coffee and moved to a window table. Dan sat down across from him. Ivan's eyes gazed out upon the boat harbor, as the wind danced across the water causing a slight chop. The first light of dawn sparkled off the rangy, snowy mountains.

"Great time of year, aye?" asked Ivan.

"Yeah, this place really gets in a guy's blood."

Ivan nodded slowly he had a thin smile on his face.

"So, what did you have on your mind, Dan?" asked Ivan, not a man for much small talk.

"Well, you know the Gull Wing. I was thinking, since old Ben is sick, that you might need someone to run her."

Ivan looked hard at Dan, as if he'd seen right through his skin.

"I might," Ivan said. "I just might." He took a husky sip of the steaming coffee. "I guess it's about time for a decision. I'll be going up to see Ben this afternoon, but when I visited him last Sunday he looked like hell."

"That's what I heard," said Dan. "It's a damn shame."

Slim put two plates, one of ham and eggs, the other, a thick pork chop and eggs, on the table, along with two heaping dishes of hash browns and a stack of buttered toast. He then poured more coffee and then sat down next to Ivan.

"I'll tell you what," said Ivan, ignoring Slim's presence, "Come and see me Friday morning. I'll have things sorted out by then . . . it's only right you know."

"I wouldn't want it any other way," Dan replied, a true sincerity to his words.

"By the way have you seen old Ben lately?" asked Ivan.

"No" said Dan.

"Do it." Said Ivan, "He was good to you."

They ate their breakfast and the conversation turned to the coming season and fish prices. In Japan, the major market for Alaskan salmon, fish prices had firmed up and Ivan indicated that his cannery would be paying top dollar. Slim and Dan smiled. Everyone in the village benefited when fish prices were high.

The next few days dragged by for Dan. He decided to do some sports fishing for the early king salmon, which had moved into the lagoon. The King was the largest of the five species of salmon and Dan was anxious to catch his first one of the season. The early May spring salmon was always the best eating. He could taste its delicate flavor. He was mighty tired of moose meat.

Friday finally arrived, and after several mugs of black coffee, Dan climbed into his dull, red parka and started for the cannery. He was early for his meeting with Ivan, so he took the long way around. As he passed by the lagoon, he saw an old sow black bear trying to do some morning fishing. She didn't even notice Dan, as he sauntered by her.

As Dan approached the cannery, his throat was parched and his shoulder muscles ached. He pulled open the worn, blue door to the office and walked down the dimly lit corridor to a shabby reception area. A cheerful, brightly dressed Indian woman sat at the front desk.

"Good morning Dan." Said Elaine, a wide smile on her round face. She was a local who had worked at the cannery forever.

"Morning Elaine, he's expecting me."

"Sure, have a seat. He's out on the dock, but he'll be back in a minute.

81

Have some coffee."

Dan followed Elaine to a dingy, lime-green storage room, which housed an enormous, commercial size coffee pot. Once the season started, the pot would brew away twenty-four hours a day seven days a week.

Elaine was taller than most Indian women. The villagers believed that she had some Russian blood in her. Several Russian families still lived in the village, all with a rich heritage. Russians founded Seldovia in the late 1700s and its name came from a Russian word, meaning herring. In those early years, herring was plentiful all through Alaska. But, they were decimated by mans' greed, just as the runs of King crab, halibut, pollack and salmon were destroyed in later years.

Ivan walked into the room.

"How're you doing, Dan?" asked Ivan, as he helped himself to the coffee. "Come on in and grab a chair."

The rectangular room had that smell of salty air and fish gurry. On the wall behind his worn desk he displayed a giant King crab. A dozen scruffy chairs lined one wall for skippers' meetings. Dan dragged a chair over near Ivan's desk.

"Care for a cigar?" asked Ivan.

"No. No thanks." Replied Dan.

Ivan unhurriedly unwrapped the Churchill-sized cigar and moistened one end of it. He looked at Dan, reached for a wooden match, struck the match and held it in the air a moment as he spoke.

"If you're the sensible type, we can make a deal on the Gull Wing."

Ivan completed lighting his cigar and inhaled it. The aroma filled the room.

Dan could hardly believe what he heard. His excitement covered his face.

"Really!' he proclaimed. "That's terrific. You bet we can strike a deal."

"Good, then I'll see if we can get an agreement drafted up for next week, if that's okay with you?" said Ivan.

"That'd be great, just great!" Dan exclaimed. "Maybe I'll have one of those cigars after all."

The next Friday, Dan and Ivan signed a contract. It was a simple deal that gave Dan and his nets, a third of the proceeds from the catch. The remaining two-thirds was to be equally divided between the crew and the boat owner. Dan believed it was a swell deal.

The following weeks were incredibly busy. He hired a crew, ordered supplies, prepared the nets and worked on the boat. He looked forward to each day and got up before dawn, anxious to get started.

The locals respected Dan and they were mighty pleased that Ivan gave the young man the opportunity. It was commonly believed that the local men were passed over for skippers from the "outside". Locals called areas beyond Alaska as the "outside".

Dan had no problems hiring a crew. They weren't all experienced deckhands, but he did recruit a seasoned cook and a reliable engineer. Dan was confident he could teach the younger men, just like Ben Jack had taught him. He had always enjoyed working with the kids on board, especially those who showed a keen interest in the fishing game.

The days flew by and on June 10th the Fish & Game Department announced that the salmon season would open the following Monday. No one in the Inlet area was surprised; it was that time of year. Dan bristled with anticipation; he and his crew had worked long and hard to get everything prepared. They were ready to go and so was the Gull Wing, with its brand-new sparkling coat of fresh paint. Dan had her painted in ivory-white, with a smart, navy-blue trim. Now, they only had to top off the fuel tanks and load their groceries aboard.

Dan was anxious to get to the fishing grounds. He wanted to scout around for fish and carefully select the area where he would be at the opening. He also would take depth soundings near certain reefs where the Sockeye salmon liked to hang out. The Sockeye was the first run to arrive each spring, in commercial quantities. They would often swing in close to the dangerous reefs. Dan could ill-afford to hang up his net on a jagged reef. He knew most of the obstacles, but he wanted to make certain. He was so intoxicated with excitement that he just plain wanted to get out of port. He had always been anxious about the start of a season, even when he was a lowly greenhorn. Now it was different, there were so many challenges being the skipper. Everything had to be considered, the fickle wind, gargantuan tides, unpredictable currents and competition from other seiners. Yet, the greatest challenge was the deceptive and cunning Sockeye itself. Of all the species, the Sockeye, which was also called Red salmon, was the cleverest of all. It was silver sleek with a blue-back and its delicate meat was a deep, blood red. When they schooled up, a single fish would often leap out of the water, its glimmering, silver skin flashing brilliantly, tempting the anxious fishermen to chase it.

The season opened Monday morning at 6:00 a.m. with a gun blast. Dan had chosen a lonesome spot, where few other boats had gathered. As he made ready to set his net for the first time as skipper, the salmon appeared everywhere. The Gull Wing was able to work on fish all day long. Set by set, hour by hour, Dan kept banging out his net. Each haul brought in abundant catches of the lucrative Sockeye. By the end of the day, the waterline had reached the gunnels of the Gull Wing. Its hatches were full of the silver creatures. None of the usual first of the season breakdowns plagued Dan. He felt blessed. His good fortune continued and each day he was thankful. Everywhere they traveled in search of fish they would find them. The crew played a major role in their success. Under Dan's strict training they operated like a finely tuned machine. The confidence Dan gained in the crew enabled him to take immense risks. He knew he would have to take risks in order to make the big catch.

Late each evening, the Gull Wing delivered its day's catch to a cannery tender. The tender boat acted as a buyer for the cannery. The tendermen would count and weigh the fish, issued fish tickets, and gave support when needed. The tender designated to the Gull Wing was always late getting back to the cannery, as Dan was the last boat to unload each night.

On Friday evenings, after fishing was closed for the week, Dan headed the Gull Wing back to Seldovia. When they arrived, dozens of fishing boats were lined up at the cannery dock, waiting impatiently to unload. The cannery purchased a lot of extra fish on Fridays, as it paid a delivery bonus of ten cents a pound. After the boats unloaded they would wash down, run into the boat harbor and tie up. The crew would hastily clean up head up to the nearest saloon. The weekend nights during the salmon season were the most profitable of the year for the cafes and bars.

It was after midnight when Dan and the Gull Wing finally unloaded their catch. While the crew cleaned up the boat, Dan walked the long, wooden-planked dock to the cannery office to pick up his fish ticket. As he was returning to the boat he met Ivan.

"You're going to be a high liner your first season." Ivan said. "Damn, you're having a hell'uva season."

Dan smiled widely and said, "Yeah, it's been pretty fair all right. I'm mighty grateful that you gave me the chance."

"Well, by God, you earned it son, and the results damn well speak for themselves.

"Thanks Ivan, "replied Dan, with a wide smile.

Ivan nodded and watched Dan as he turned and with long, young, strides made his way back down the dock.

Dan jumped aboard the Gull Wing, yelled at the crew to release the lines and in a moment they pulled away from the dock. He sped over to the small boat harbor, ignoring the "no wake" signs prominently posted. They moved into their berth and before the Gull Wing was fully secured, the crew, with duffel bags slung over their shoulders, headed ashore. Dan smiled to himself. He remembered those nights, when he could hardly wait to hit town.

This night however, he was dead tired and he lay down on his bunk, intending to rest a moment. He didn't awake until nearly 6 a.m., a few minutes after the last crewman had staggered aboard.

Towards the end of August heavy rains poured down on Cook Inlet prompting the silvery salmon to head for fresh water. Each autumn, Mother Nature called for the mature salmon to return to the river or stream of its birth, to procreate and then die.

In early September, Dan brought the Gull Wing into port for the last time. Seldovia was all a buzz with the rich success Dan, a rookie skipper, had achieved. Later that night Dan found himself up at the Inn, the favorite watering hole of the local skippers. It was traditional for the high liners to buy rounds for the house. Dan bought his first rounds. The patrons, nearly all fisher people, believed it would be a tradition young Dan would participate in for many future years. Dan was embarrassed by all the attention that he was being paid. Everyone in the bar talked about him.

"First year luck," some of the skippers mused.

"Just a lot of fish this season," said others.

"A damned good fisherman," explained Ivan.

Fall comes quickly in Alaska and departs even faster, making way for the hard winter. The rains that started in late August continued through September. But in late September they were accompanied by bitter cold and nasty, high winds. In early October the village had its first dusting of snow.

The local gossip had it that there would be a limited King crab season in November. After the successful salmon season, a crab opening would significantly boost Seldovia's fragile economy. All the villagers were excited about this possibility.

Ivan was leaving for the "outside" in a few days and Dan needed to talk with him. He hurried down to the cannery, a familiar walk by now.

"Hi Dan," greeted Elaine. "Go right in. He's alone."

"Thanks, you're looking mighty fine this morning."

Blushing, Elaine lowered her head as Dan walked into Ivan's office, smiling to himself.

"Well good morning Dan," said Ivan, as he got up to shake the hand of his newest high liner. "Miserable damn day, huh?"

"Sure is," replied Dan.

"Are we all settled up from the season?"

"You bet and thanks again," said Dan, as he sat down. "I wanted to talk with you about taking the Gull Wing out for crab.

Ivan leaned back in his chair, reached for a cigar, and offered Dan one, without saying a word. Dan shook his head. The large-framed cannery boss looked dead serious.

"I figured you'd be coming around," said Ivan. "I did some serious thinking about it. You're a damned good skipper and you've been around the sea a number of years, but you've never fished crab and it's a whole different ball game in the winter. I know you're young and full of get-up, but by God that sea out there is treacherous in the winter." Ivan made a motion toward the window with his huge hand, paused a moment and put a match to his cigar.

Ivan rose from his desk and walked to the double-paned window, and looked out on the Inlet. Vast green waves pounded at the pilings, supporting the cannery dock. He shook his head ponderously, and turned to face the young skipper.

"Dan, I want to urge you to first get a couple years of winter experience under your belt. When you do that, you know, I'll support you 100 percent," said Ivan. The message was delivered with affection.

"I hear you Ivan, and I appreciate what you're saying. It makes good sense. I'll see who I can get a deck job with," replied Dan, his disappointment not evident.

"That's good, it shows a hell of a lot of maturity," said Ivan. "And, believe me any skipper would welcome you aboard. Your stock is damn high right now." Ivan gave one of his rare smiles, his relief was obvious.

As the two men shook hands, Ivan explained that he would be going "outside" for a couple weeks. He told Dan that if he needed anything to let Elaine know. Dan nodded and left Ivan's office. He didn't say a word to Elaine, as he passed her desk.

It was a gray, blustery day, as Dan left the cannery. The piercing north wind blew fiercely against his face. He was in a gloomy mood and decided that he'd drive over to Jakolof Bay. The tail end of the fall Silver run was in and he wanted to try his luck catching one with his new fiber glass pole. He could also think better out on the sea.

Over the summer he didn't have much time to himself. It had been a thrilling season and he had worked his 'keister' off but he loved every minute of it. He had longed to skipper his own boat and he finally achieved his dream. Now he had to sort out the advice Ivan had given him.

Ivan departed Seldovia the next morning and each day he checked in with Elaine. Three days before he was scheduled to return, Elaine called him in a panic. She informed Ivan that Dan had agreed to run a crab boat, the Sea Wolf, for a cannery in Homer. A frightening chill ran down Ivan's spine, he knew the Sea Wolf. It was another old rig, but unlike the Gull Wing, she had not been well maintained. It was a converted, wooden purse seiner from Puget Sound, built around 1910 and not suitable for the rigors of King crab fishing. Ivan also remembered that the Sea Wolf didn't have refrigeration, which meant Dan would have to unload his catch each day or risk the crab dying. The canneries were prohibited from purchasing dead crab.

"God damn it," Ivan cried out loud to no one.

The Coast Guard regulations allowed anything that floated to get a fishing permit. Only greed governed and it made no sense at all. Commercial fishing in Alaska was the most hazardous business in America. Operating with a vessel like the Sea Wolf was impossible. It wasn't simply risky, it was just plain crazy.

When Ivan arrived back in Seldovia Elaine told him that Dan already loaded his pots and left port. Ivan's mouth was parched and his heart was racing. He checked with several charter services in hopes of getting someone to take him out to search for the Sea Wolf, but the weather was too severe. Even the most experienced pilots refused. The risk of going up in an Alaskan blizzard was too perilous.

All that day Ivan sat by his bank of ship-to-shore radios trying to make contact with the Sea Wolf. Yet, he knew that it was impossible to make radio contact into certain areas around the Inlet. Dan and the Sea Wolf were in one of those areas. Ivan was furious and his stomach was acid-filled. Despite the hopelessness he felt in his gut, he continued his watch. Hour after hour he attempted, in vain, to reach the Sea Wolf.

When the black night arrived Ivan still hadn't reached the Sea Wolf. He had smoked half-dozen cigars and drank several mugs of coffee. At 10:00 p.m. the daily catch reports started rolling in from his crabbers. None of the boats that checked in had caught much of a catch. Ivan wasn't surprised with the lousy, rotten weather they'd been experiencing. Yet, he knew that top skippers seldom, if ever, called in with their tally.

Ivan inquired of every boat he could raise as to whether they had seen the Sea Wolf. No one knew where Dan had ventured. It was typical, everyone was concerned with his own problems and the severe weather caused skippers to be on edge.

By midnight Ivan was dog-tired and decided to go home. He tried sleeping, but he couldn't get Dan out of his thoughts. After tossing around for a couple hours, he got up and returned to the cannery. It was well before dawn and only Raul, the one-armed, night janitor was there. He had worked for Ivan for over twenty years and saw that his boss was troubled.

"Good morning boss," said Raul, always solicitous and polite toward Ivan. "You're here so early."

"Yeah, couldn't sleep," replied Ivan. "Gotta keep trying to raise Dan."

"Yes, boss, keep trying. You'll reach him."

Ivan nodded, headed to the radio shack and started calling. He didn't take off either his parka or cap.

"Hello the Sea Wolf, the Sea Wolf, the Sea Wolf. This is 89905 Seldovia, do you read Dan?"

Ivan stared down at the tiny microphone in his bear sized hands. There was no response. He tried again.

"Calling the Sea Wolf, the Sea Wolf, this is Seldovia. Do you read me Dan'?"

Ivan paused a minute, sweat lines dotted his wrinkled brow. He threw off his heavy parka and marched into his office. He grabbed a cigar from a drawer and sat down in his ample sized, black, leather chair. His cap still on, he rested his head back. The big man's eyes were moist.

Suddenly, Ivan jumped up when he heard a familiar voice on the radio. Blackie reported that he had caught a few. Ivan smiled thinly; he knew that when Blackie reported that he had a few that it meant that he had probably loaded down his boat with crab. Blackie said that he had seen the Sea Wolf heading across the Inlet towards Homer and that the wind was howling like hell with gusts up to sixty knots. Ivan wasn't surprised; it was typical weather for this time of the year. He knew that Dan would be bucking the tide, in addition to fighting typhoon like winds. Ivan tried calling the Sea Wolf again but to no avail. He plopped himself down on a wooden bench near the radio. He chewed on his cigar, which he hadn't got around to lighting.

In the meantime, the Sea Wolf had lain at anchor for nearly fifteen hours, waiting for the winds to subside. But calm never came and the raging storm showed no signs of letting up. Dan walked the cramped bridge of the Sea Wolf for what seemed like days. The more he walked the more impatient he became. He realized that he didn't have much time to make a decision. The crab had gotten docile and showed little life. Dan knew if they didn't immediately start for the cannery the crab would be dead by the time they arrived.

The Sea Wolf was plugged to its gunnels with crab and the canneries were paying $2.00 per pound. The same good fortune that blessed Dan during the salmon season was still shining on him. He had 100 grand worth of crab in his hold and he wasn't about to lose it. He believed in his heart, he could somehow make it across the Inlet. If the storm proved to be too severe, he'd simply turn the Sea Wolf around. He ordered his crew to raise the anchor.

The crewmen looked at each other in dismay, as they checked all the fastenings and secured the hatches. The Sea Wolf moved cautiously out of its safe harbor. Off in the far distance, the harsh sea and sky merged appearing smoky and violent. Dan grabbed the wheel topside, his body ached and his throat was cotton-dry. The unkind wind was blustery and the icy rain chilled him to the bone. As the Sea Wolf pulled around the cape and into the open sea, they were hit with a mountain-high swell. It swept right through them. Dan momentarily lost his balance, as blue water filled the decks and swooped down the gunnels. He regained his equilibrium and braced himself gripping the spokes of the wheel with all the strength he could muster. As the violent storm surrounded them, each successive wave was higher and more crushing. Dan couldn't comprehend such raw force. He had experienced several violent storms, yet nothing compared with this.

As each massive wave hit, the bow of the Sea Wolf careened high into the air, only to crash down with unrelenting force. When the rudder and propeller protruded out of the water Dan was powerless, yet he didn't despair. He intently watched every movement of the sea, desperately trying to remember everything that he had learned. Firmly he planted his boots on the deck, as his body molded with the wheel. Again and again the Sea Wolf's old bow dipped into the abyss, only to rise again, fiercely thrusting them into a black and ugly trough between the waves. Dan felt control being snatched away, as he struggled with every ounce of energy he could muster. And then the Sea Wolf failed to respond. Warm urine dribbled down the side of his leg. He tried backing off on the throttle, but it was no help. He was powerless. He pleaded to God for intercession.

It felt that they had been in the storm forever, yet it had been barely an hour. Dan's fingers had already cramped, from the stranglehold grip he had on the wheel, and his nose was numb from the sub-zero temperature. The ice-rain clung to his beard making him a ghoulish sight.

"Come on ol' girl" screamed Dan. "Get us across this God forsaken sea."

Dan knew it was impossible to turn the Sea Wolf around without foundering. He had to keep the bow into the oncoming sea. It would be a great risk to turn and put the sea amidships. Their only chance of surviving would be if the wind subsided, as the tide changed, an unlikely turn of events.

Soon it would be nightfall and Dan recalled these long, Alaskan, winter nights. He vigilantly watched each measure of the sea, as the torrential ocean pounded them. Dan wondered how long the Sea Wolf could endure this cruelty. Relentlessly, the narrow bow of the vessel sliced into the impetuous waves, digging through with unfettered defiance. The ancient craft climbed up each approaching wave only to come crashing back down into the bottomless ravine. Dan could hear the spine of the Sea Wolf creaking and moaning. It was a morbid, complaining cry.

Dan prayed like he never had before. He regretted that he hadn't gone "outside" to see his folks before the season started. He hadn't even seen his kid sister's new son. His life, for the past few years, had been fishing. The deep had calmed him after all the death and pain of Vietnam. He remembered how he feared death when his squadron had been ambushed. Life was so fragile and the sea, like war, seldom gave second chances.

As Dan searched the sea, his eyes shifted off to the port side. There coming at us, the inexplicable errant wave. He recalled Ben Jack's story of the devil swell, a Titanic wave that left no survivors. Now it was less than 50 fathoms away, its mass cruising directly at the Sea Wolf with staggering speed. It dwarfed the other towering waves they had been combating. Impatiently, it surged, engulfing the Sea Wolf, as if it were a toy. The mammoth wave picked up the Sea Wolf, on its blue-green crest, and threw her down and trampled her old bones.

The sea conquered and Dan was only a witness. He could hear the wretched screams of his crew, as he lost his footing and began his own deathly slide. He scratched and clawed at the decking, desperately trying to gain a foothold.

He lunged at a guy-wire, just as the Sea Wolf went into its very last roll.

The frigid, seawater encompassed him, as he drifted through its depths. The acrid taste of the salt water was the last thing he remembered.

The Sea Wolf continued its roll and tumbled into the depths of oblivion settling into her permanent interment.

Fort Casey

Autumn afternoon
on South Whidbey,
tide slack, wind a murmur
as short choppy waves break
on the welcoming shore.

Far-off a toy-like ferry
chugs across the Sound.
And near the far shore,
a royal blue hulled trawler
heads toward its homeport
to anxious families
after months in Bering Sea.
The sun sets a fiery glow
on its steel skin.

Walking among the bone-colored
drift wood and dried kelp
a hooked nosed chum salmon
flops near the water's edge,
a puzzling sign.

Across the desolate Straits
flicking incandescent
lights of Port Townsend.
The sun makes its fading ritual
behind the merciless Olympic Mountains
as burnt-orange shadows ignite,
stirring old memories.

Lupine

Leaving the Aleutians flying high
not a cloud in the cobalt sky.
Soaring and drifting like an eagle,
feeling strangely very regal.

Above the mountains thick with ice,
far below a sun-drenched crevice
flush with Lupine in grand array
swarms of lusty Lupine in early May
their tapering spikes of blue and white
pointing at heaven like guns of fright.

And when dreaming today I remember still
that bolt from the blue and nature's thrill.

F/V Veribus

— RECIPES —

The following recipes are a sampling of the dishes that were often prepared on the fishing boats. We were privileged to have cooks from numerous countries such as Italy, Germany, Brazil, Portugal and Latvia. Each had his own special cuisine from his native country. Yet these men gave me a respect for the foods that we prepare.

Even though there was not a big emphasis on balanced diet they always provided a sensible variety of meat, fish, vegetables and fruit. And they all were generous with olive oil, tomatoes, garlic and red wine. It was Mediterranean cuisine before we were aware in America of such a thing. Yet their main purpose was to make their food full of flavor and filling for the fishermen who performed grueling work eighteen hours a day.

Some of these recipes are elemental but others are unique to the territory:

BAKED WHITE SALMON   *Serves 6*

The White King salmon is a rarity. They seldom reach 30 pounds and are found only in a few rivers in Puget Sound and Alaska. It was my grandfather's absolute favorite fish and the one he would always take home to his family on weekends. Its deliciousness comes from its fat content (naturally fatty acids) which is significantly greater than the Red King and other species of salmon. The added good fat content (omega—3s) generally means that the fish had to travel long distances to reach its spawning grounds. On the Columbia, Yukon, and Copper Rivers salmon must travel over a thousand miles. Since Salmon don't feed while in fresh water they depend on this fat to provide the energy to reach their final destination.

One summer, on the Veribus, Grandpa Tasovac, while we were pulling in the seine spotted a white King in the net. He speared it, dragged it in, pulled it aboard and had it filleted in three minutes flat. He gave it over to the cook who ran it to the galley and threw it on the grill. By the time we had the net aboard and secure the cook had the fish grilled and laid out on the hatch ready to eat. That is fresh fish!

INGREDIENTS:

3 pound center cut salmon roast

3 stalks of celery

1 Onion

1 Lemon

6 cloves of garlic

Salt & pepper

Place fish in a shallow baking pan surrounded by a few stalks of celery. After thoroughly salting and peppering, stuff the cavity of the fish with garlic and onion. Rub the juice of one lemon over the body of the fish and lightly cover with foil. Bake in 350-degree oven for about 30 minutes. It is a sin to overcook this delightful fish and remember that ovens often vary in temperature.

FRIED CLAMS *Serves 6*

The most enjoyable part of preparing any clam dish was the adventure of digging the clams. In Alaska the sweet butter clam was in great abundance. When fishing with FB we would go clam digging in Idaho Inlet in Icy Straits. We would anchor the Cypress and someone would take two or three of us in the skiff to the beach. And within an hour we would easily have 30 pounds of the finest tasting clams imaginable. We would take them back to the seiner and put them into gunnysacks filled with corn meal, toss them over the side and let them soak for five or six hours. Overnight is better. This would clean them out and rid them of any sand particles. Sand is not good.

INGREDIENTS:

Two pounds of clean clam meat

½ cup ordinary flour

Salt, pepper and garlic powder

Olive oil

Mix the flour, salt, pepper and garlic powder in a paper bag and place the clams in the bag vigorously shaking it.

Prepare the frying pan by adding two tablespoons of olive oil. Place on medium high heat. Add the clams making certain to shake off any excess flour.

Cook quickly about three minutes on each side in a frying pan or about two minutes on a grill. Longer cooking time will result in tough and chewy clams.

We would usually serve this dish with a big tossed green salad and French bread.

SPAGHETTI WITH OXTAILS IN TOMATO SAUCE
Serves 10 hungry fishermen

This is my favorite pasta sauce recipe. It is delightfully tasty with rich flavors and a hearty texture drawn from these carefully chosen ingredients. You need to make a fairly sizable portion because dainty just plain doesn't work. I have tried small portions and it doesn't taste like I remembered it. It should be served over the heaviest pasta such as rigatoni, mostaccioli or bucatina.

My mother always liked to mix 50% rigatoni with 50% spaghetti or bucatina. If you do that be sure that once the water starts to boil that you put the rigatoni in the water three minutes before you put in the spaghetti or bucatina.

Often times when I was skippering I would give my cook Sunday off and I would do the cooking. One Sunday, we were traveling to new fishing grounds, and I told John Armenia I would cook. I prepared this dish. When it was finished, I told the crew to come and eat. Since we were traveling, I went up to the pilothouse and relieved the crewman at the wheel so he could eat with the rest of the crew. Thirty minutes or so later, I returned to the galley to have my meal. There was not an iota of anything left. The crew consumed every last bit of the pasta, sauce and meat. It even looked like someone wiped the kettle clean with some French bread. I was not a happy skipper.

INGREDIENTS:

6 tablespoons of olive oil

6-8 medium to large sized oxtails. Make sure they are fresh and that the fat, which interlaces the bone, is a bright fresh white color

One pound of ground beef

One pound of ground pork

3 pound beef roast cut into 3 inch pieces

2 cups of diced onions

10 cloves of garlic

4—1 pound cans of a good quality tomato sauce

4 oz. of tomato paste

1 cup of chopped parsley

1 tablespoon of dried oregano

2 teaspoons of freshly ground pepper

Zest from one orange

Juice from the orange

2 tablespoons of sugar

1 cup of dry red wine

½ pound of parmiggiano (freshly shaved)

Heat on low two tablespoons of the olive oil in a large heavy frying pan and add four cloves of garlic. This should take about two or three minutes. Add the oxtails and brown lightly on each side say about 5-7 minutes.

In the meantime, you can be sautéing the onion and the rest of the garlic in another frying pan using the same amount of olive oil as above. When the onions are translucent, place them in a large, heavy-duty saucepan. (I have a big old iron pot that I have from the Whitworth, the seiner that I skippered in the sixties. It must be nearly 100 years old.) Add the canned tomato sauce, paste, salt, pepper and oregano, orange juice and peel. Let simmer at medium heat while the meat is browning. As the oxtails are browned, place them in the sauce.

Then brown the beef roast the same way and add it to the sauce. Finally, when the beef is done, brown the ground beef and ground pork for about 10-12 minutes. (Make sure you drain the fat from the skillet each time you brown the other meats).

Place the ground meat on a paper towel to drain the grease and then add this to the sauce as well. Add the parsley, salt to taste and let the sauce simmer. I usually let it simmer for about four hours. Check and taste the sauce periodically adding the red wine and a little more salt if needed. The sauce is best tasted by placing it in a small bowl accompanied by a piece of fresh French bread for dipping.

Bring the water to a boil and add the pasta. When it is al dente drain the water and place back into the pot, add the sauce, some cheese and let sit for

5 minutes. The key according to one of our Italian cooks was to make sure that there was not excess sauce in the bottom of the pan.

You will have plenty of sauce left over. It keeps very well in the freezer and many a night it came in handy when guests drop in for a quick meal.

This serves 10 hungry fishermen; it would probably serve 20 normal eating people. As the dinner hour approaches, prepare your pasta of choice. When the pasta is al dente, drain using the hot water to warm the bowl that you will be using to serve the pasta. I love the pasta the next day. It seems to have an even better taste as the spaghetti (or whatever pasta you choose) inhales the sauce.

This hearty meal calls for a big, rich Cabernet or Sangiovese. When we are really celebrating we will choose an Italian Barolo, Barbaresco or Brunello di Montalcino. These are also known as the "Killer B's". Great!

GRILLED ALASKAN KING SALMON

Grandpa Tasovac's Specialty   *Serves 6*

First, I must relate a little history and background on the five common species of salmon. They are:

The Chum, Keta or Dog salmon is very plentiful in Alaska waters. In Puget Sound they are called chum, in British Columbia Keta and in Alaska Dogs. It is the last specie to be harvested in the fall of the year. In Puget Sound they are caught up through Thanksgiving. The average size is 8 pounds. This specie is not considered the best eating and traditionally it was either canned or smoked. Today it is still smoked but also sold in the frozen state as silverbrites, albeit they are a far cry from silver. They are of good quality if caught bright. In the fall when they start turning a burnt orange color their meat quality quickly deteriorates. This occurs when they come into fresh water. Chum Salmon get their name Dog Salmon from their enormous protruding teeth and large hooked nose. They are also used extensively to feed sled dogs. Keta is an Indian name for the chum salmon. In the late fall we would sell the last of the season's catch to several local dog trainers in and around the Anchorage area.

Alaska Pink salmon are very plentiful throughout Alaska from Southeastern to Central from Kodiak to the Alaskan Peninsula. They tend to be small with most weighing in less than three pounds. Their meat is soft when they move into the inland waters. Traditionally they were used primarily for canning however, in recent years a large percentage is frozen for the retail market. The modern housewife or house-husband is not enamored with canned fish. There simply are too many other options that allow the consumer to have fresh or fresh frozen nearly year round. In Puget Sound Pink salmon are called humpbacks for the pronounced hump they develop when they come into fresh water. This is by far the most prolific species and remains the backbone of the purse seine fleet in Alaska.

Coho or silver salmon are widespread but are limited in number in Alaska waters. Generally only 2 or 3 percent of our total catch on the seiners were Coho. They are a great eating fish and are the most popular with sport fishermen. Charter boats on the coast in Washington and Oregon depend on strong runs in order to attract their annual customers to places like Ilwaco, Forks and Westport, Washington. They are strong fighters in saltwater and in streams. They range in size from 10 pounds to 12 pounds but often they reach 20 pounds. Coho are also called Silver Salmon due to their bright blue-silver color. In the commercial fisheries world they are known as incidental catch and there was never an established market due to the minimum quantities available.

Alaska Red (Sockeye) Salmon are the crown prince of the family of salmon. They are prolific in some Alaska waters, such as Bristol Bay but are rare in many others. Their flesh is blood red and they average 5- 6 pounds in Alaska and over 7 pounds in Puget Sound. They are the rich in fatty acids (omega-3s) and therefore need little seasoning when broiling or barbequing their luscious flesh.

In Alaska the Sockeye is called Red Salmon and in Puget Sound they are called Sockeye. Sockeye are also called "money fish" by the fishermen for reasons I mentioned in the narrative.

King or Chinook are the largest of all salmon. They are the first salmon of the season to come into rivers in the spring to spawn. In recent years these early fish fetch a handsome price per pound. When I had the Cordova plant in the late 1960's we paid about $1.00 per fish and they averaged over 20 pounds with some well above 50 pounds. Today retailers charge $20.00 to $30.00 per pound for the early catch in late April and early May. They are also a great sportsmen's attraction as they fight very hard and their size makes them a significant challenge to land. Chinook are called King salmon due to their size. And of all the species it is absolutely the best eating and it is easy to prepare.

INGREDIENTS:

½ cup olive oil

4 garlic cloves, finely chopped

salt and pepper

Handful of finely chopped fresh parsley

Select a fresh, wild, preferably a White King salmon, #3 filet

On the boat we always prepared this delectable fish immediately after taking it from the net. And that is fresh. Unfortunately, most of you will never know fresh salmon like that.

Simple is the key to great fish preparation. The flavor of the fish is enhanced by restraining your use of sauces and spices. I urge you to use nothing more than a little garlic powder, salt, pepper, and lemon.

On Friday evenings, Grandpa would fix this preparation and Grandma Palma enhanced it with fresh fried potatoes and zayah, a preparation of spinach, red potatoes, zucchini and horse beans (fava beans) tossed with olive oil and salt and pepper.

Use as many filets or steaks as are required for the number of guests that you are serving. Guests often eat more when the salmon is prepared this way. Remember the fish is terrific cold in salads and sandwiches.

First, brush the grill generously with olive oil.

Second, brush the fish with a combination of olive oil and pepper.

Place salmon on the grill, skin side up, for 5-7 minutes. Then turn each piece over and cook until the fish flakes about 3-4 minutes. Salt lightly. This presumes the thickness of each piece of the fish is ¾ of an inch. Don't overcook. Overcooking is the number one reason why fish becomes dry and loses flavor.

Remove from grill and sprinkle with fresh parsley

I have taken the best of the many recipes that I have tasted over the years. Each cook had his own way of preparing this standard fare. In the old days, on the fishing boats, we had soup every day for our mid-day meal. It was hearty, nutritious and very tasty. Generally, we would first have a bowl or two of the soup, which included pasta such as macaroni, penne or conchiglie. If you are in a hurry you can use vermicelli, which cooks up very quickly. After we finished the soup the cook would bring on a giant platter of the meat and vegetables including potatoes, carrots, celery and onions. Often the old men (they were probably in their fifties) would have one glass of red wine, which they would fetch from the wine barrel, which was lashed, to the port side of the bow.

INGREDIENTS:

4 pounds of short ribs, neck bones or a beef roast. The key is whatever you use there must be some bones that are included. Julia was 100% correct about the bones.

2 large onions, quartered

3-4 ribs of celery, roughly chopped

6-8 carrots, whole

4-6 potatoes, quartered

Handful of chopped parsley

1 16-ounce can of tomato sauce

Salt and pepper to taste

Place the meat in cold, salted water (about 4 quarts) in a large stockpot. Bring it to a boil and skim off the froth that comes to the top of the water. Add the onions, quartered, the tomato sauce, carrots, celery and parsley. Cook for two hours and then add the potatoes and cook for another 30 minutes. Test the broth for taste and add more salt and pepper as needed. Strain the broth and keep the meat and vegetables warm.

To the boiling broth add your pasta of choice and cook for about 12–14 minutes (except the vermicelli which takes about one-half the time)

This is another hearty and tasty soup. My son Matt loved split pea soup and I made it often for him when he was in school.

Benny Calacino, our cook on the F/V Cypress, would make a great pot of split pea soup and just let it simmer on the back of the oil fueled marine stove. By the end of the day, it would be consumed by the crew as they passed through the galley.

INGREDIENTS:

2—8oz packages of split peas

1 large dry onion, diced

Large bone from picnic ham or 2½ pounds of ham hocks

1.5 pounds of ham meat from the picnic ham

4 carrots, chopped

2 stalks of celery, chopped

Wash the peas as per the instructions on package and place in large stock pot. Add water, the ham bone(s), diced onion, carrots and the celery with leaves. Add salt and pepper to taste. Bring to boil again and add the ham meat then turn to low and leave it be for at least four hours. Test occasionally for taste. Add salt & pepper as needed.

Serve with good quality saltine crackers. It is a filling and satisfying meal.

As soon as we would make our first stop in southeastern Alaska, usually Warm Springs Bay, the fishing lines were tossed overboard. Whatever was caught would go into the fish soup. Generally, it was a halibut, codfish or snapper. I personally preferred a rich, king salmon. However, the first year I fished in Alaska we stopped in Warm Springs Bay and I was the first to return to the boat from taking a hot bath at the springs. So, I naturally threw out a line. In just a few minutes I had hooked what felt to be the bottom. Captain Rudolfo, the skipper of the St. Bernadette came over to see what I had on my line. Together we pulled up a 220-pound halibut. We cleaned it, cut it up and distributed it to all of the boats in the harbor. All the fleet enjoyed it.

INGREDIENTS:

3 pounds of cut-up (serving size) fresh fish fillets

4 quarts of cold water

2 cloves of garlic

2 tablespoons of parsley, chopped

1 cup celery, diced

2 medium onions, quartered.

3 pounds potatoes, quartered

2 pounds carrots, chopped

5 garlic cloves, crushed

⅓ cup olive oil

16 oz. can tomato sauce

Salt and pepper to taste

Sauté the onions and garlic in olive oil in a large, heavy kettle. Add the water and all other ingredients but the fish. Cook for 60 minutes, add the fish and cook simmer for 15 minutes. Take out the fish and vegetables and keep warm in the oven. Add rice or pasta to the broth and cook until done.

Gnocchi was not a dish that was served often on the boats. The preparation took too long for the cook who had three meals and a couple of mug ups already to prepare. (A mug up is a quick in between meal that gave the crew some added sustenance when they were working long hours when the fish were in abundance). Having gnocchi was generally a celebration meal, like hitting the 100,000 mark, loading down the boat or maybe heading for home.

INGREDIENTS:

4 cups mashed potatoes (6 large potatoes)

3 eggs

1 cup flour

1 tablespoon of butter

2 teaspoons of olive oil

1 cup fresh Parmesan cheese

2 cups spaghetti sauce

Boil potatoes until tender, drain and then mash your potatoes until light and fluffy add butter. When cooled add the eggs one at a time and beat the mixture well. Work the flour in slowly until all has been added and the mixture is smooth but slightly sticky.

Boil salted water and add the olive oil.

Take the dough and divide into fourths. Roll out each piece into a fifteen-inch rope about½ inch in diameter. Cut each rope into about 25 pieces. Drop the njoki into the boiling water. When the njoki rise to the surface, cook for about one minute and then drain. Add the spaghetti sauce and shave the fresh Parmesan cheese and distribute generously. Cover for 15 minutes and serve.

The old timers would simply enjoy the njoki with melted butter and Parmesan.

The Italians are well known for their Cioppino and the French for their Bouillabaisse. However, this Croatian fish stew will not take a back seat to either. Of course, Croatia is across the Adriatic Sea from Italy and many spices and recipes became intermingled. So no one knows for certain the origination of many of the recipes that we think of coming from old Europe.

Again and again I talk about freshness. Well the reason the French Bouillabaisse lacks the same flavor and richness as the Cioppino from Italy or Croatia is that they don't have the same abundant fresh fish. This is the famous rainy day noon meal. I remember enjoying it at a little hole in the wall restaurant on fishermen's wharf in San Francisco in the early 60's when I was attending Santa Clara. I think we got a jug of wine, a loaf of bread, a salad and a huge bowl of Cioppino for $1.95. Maybe a desert was tossed in as well.

INGREDIENTS:

1 quart of manila or steamer clams

1 cups red wine

2 Dungeness crab, (cleaned and cracked) and broken into pieces

1 pound of shrimp (preferably 16 counts, which means simply 16 to a pound) Shrimp are seldom found fresh as they come primarily from Mexico or China. However, most producers do a very good job and if the vendor has thawed them properly they will do just fine. The other option is to buy them frozen and thaw them yourself. Not a big job.

½ cup olive oil

1 large onion, chopped

4 garlic cloves, chopped

1 green pepper, chopped

1 red pepper, chopped

4 tomatoes peeled and chopped

1 6-ounce can of tomato paste

1 quart calm juice

2 cups red wine

Salt and pepper to taste

1 teaspoon dried basil

3 pounds sea bass, red rockfish, salmon, halibut

Steam the clams with one cup of wine until they open. Discard any clams that don't open.

Remove the shells. Strain the broth and reserve. Break the crab into pieces. (Normally the fishmonger will do this for you). Heat the olive oil in a large pot and add the onion, green pepper, and garlic for three minutes. Add the tomatoes and cook for another 5 minutes. Add the clam broth, tomato paste and red wine. Season to taste. Cook for 20-30 minutes and check for taste. Add the basil and then the finfish. When the fish is still firm, after about 5 minutes, add the clams, the crab and shrimp. It is easy to tell when the shell fish are done as the shrimp will turn an orange-red color. Don't overcook as it takes away the flavor and fish becomes mushy. Sprinkle with parsley.

Again, crusty bread, green salad and a hearty wine like a French Burgundy make this a special treat.

I fished with Francis Barcott on the FV Cypress in the summers of 1955 to 1957 and again in 1960. He was the ultimate salmon skipper. He was Croatian and was raised on fishing boats and learning from his father. Francis was an epicurean before the word was commonly used. I was especially fortunate to develop a passion and respect for good food from F.B. In addition to being my captain, he was a father figure to me and someone I loved and admired. Besides enjoying the preparation of the food, we had a great time catching the crabs, clams, octopus and halibut.

The clams were in such abundance that we would often pull into Idaho Inlet, which is located in Icy Straits a few miles before the Inian Islands, and in sight of an hour we would lower the skiff, go to the beach and dig 100 pounds of the most mouth-watering butter clams that you could ever find. I figured that there were 3 to 4 pounds of mature clams per square foot. I did a minor study of the beaches in Idaho Inlet which resulted in my writing a term paper on the harvesting and availability of clams in Southeastern Alaska.

So here is F.B.'s recipe as I remember it.

INGREDIENTS:

3-5 pounds of potatoes, diced

1 quart of clam nectar

½ pound of thick bacon

Handful of parsley

2 pounds of clam meat

1 large onion, rough chopped

5 garlic cloves, chopped,

2 quarts of whole milk, not skimmed

Cube of butter

Salt and pepper to taste

In a frying pan brown the bacon in olive oil with 5 garlic cloves. Set aside. Brown the onion. Add the diced potatoes, clam nectar and butter to the onion and cook until the potatoes are done.

Place the bacon, onion and potatoes in a heavy-duty pot and add the clams, milk, and seasoning. Cook for 3-5 minutes at low heat. Serve piping hot with saltine crackers, add pepper and a dollop of butter to each bowl. Enjoy and thanks F.B.

SPRING LAMB STEW

This is one of my top five favorite entrees. When prepared properly it is as savory a dish that you can serve. The richness of the flavors is gained by the use of the freshest ingredients coupled with long slow, cooking time at very low heat.

There are several cuts of lamb that you can use. However, the key is that whatever cut you use you must have some bones such as the neck, shoulder or leg. This will provide the kind of sauce that makes this dish exceptional. The other key is the variety of vegetables. The three root vegetables are found in most supermarkets.

INGREDIENTS:

3 pounds of lamb, cut into 3 oz. pieces

2 tablespoons of olive oil

1 cup flour

4 cloves of garlic minced

6 carrots, chopped

2 onions, rough chopped

1 rutabaga, chopped

1 turnip, chopped

2 parsnips, chopped

4-6 red potatoes, halved

2 stalks of celery, diced

8—10 oz. of tomato sauce

16 oz. beef broth

2 cups of red wine

2 cups green peas—fresh or frozen

Dredge the lamb in flour, salt and pepper. Shake off the excess flour. Heat the olive oil in a heavy frying pan and sauté the lamb until browned on all sides. Set aside.

Sauté the garlic, the celery and chopped onion in a large heavy kettle. Add the meat, tomato sauce and one cup of wine and simmer for one hour.

Add the remaining vegetables (except for the peas)and turn the heat up until it starts to boil, reduce heat and simmer for another two hours. Continue to simmer and in the last 15 minutes add another cup of wine and the peas.

Serve this with very crusty bread, a light green salad with oil and vinegar and a solid Pinot Noir from Oregon or the Central Coast of California.

FISH BRUDET–DALMATIAN STYLE

This is a dish that can be made with nearly any type of fish. I favor the white fish and since Halibut is very available in the northwest I often choose that. It is also great with snapper, ling or true cod or monk fish.

INGREDIENTS:

8 pieces @ 4 ounces each of any fish mentioned above.

2 medium onions—roughly chopped

½ Cup finely chopped parsley

⅓ Cup olive oil

1 large can whole tomatoes

2 bay leaves, remove after cooking

5 crushed garlic cloves

½ teaspoon oregano

¼ cup vinegar

1 cup of a heavy red wine (we used a homemade wine taken from the barrel secured on the port side near the bow)

Sauté the onion and garlic in the olive oil. Add the remainder of the ingredients, except for the fish and place in the heavy kettle (if you have one) If not use the sturdiest pot that you own. Bring everything to a slow boil for 10 to 15 minutes. Add the fish and turn the heat to low or simmer. When the fish is tender to the touch of the fork (this probably means about 5 to 7 minutes) the meal is ready.

Serve with rustic bread, a green salad with oil and vinegar dressing and a crispy, dry and green white wine such as Chenin Blanc, Sauvignon Blanc or Pinot Grigio.

AN AMISH DISH

Serves 4-6

No, we didn't ever have an Amish cook. However, we had a German cook in the early fifties who had spent time with Amish relatives in Pennsylvania. This dish was a big hit with the crew and one I have savored over the years. It is a favorite of my wife Susan and when I am doing the cooking she often requests this hearty and flavorful meal.

The cook who prepared this dish was a crusty and sort of mean old guy. He wasn't the most salubrious of cooks and that really bothered my shipmate and friend Bob Barcott. One afternoon Bob went into galley to make a sandwich and when he opened the bread drawer he found loaves of moldy bread. Bob had a temper; he yelled out a few expletives, pulled out the drawer and proceeded to throw the bread and the drawer overboard. F.B. was enraged both at Bob and the cook. Fortunately the drawer floated and we were able to retrieve it. Clearly there was never any more moldy bread in that galley.

INGREDIENTS:

6-8 potatoes, boiled

1-quart sauerkraut

1 rack of lean pork ribs

½ cup milk, warmed

2 Tablespoons of butter

Salt/pepper

Paprika

While the potatoes are boiling, cut up the ribs and place them in cold water in a pot, bringing them to a rapid boil. This will remove a great deal of the fat.

Mash the potatoes adding the warm milk and butter. Then place a layer of the potatoes in an ovenproof pan followed by a layer of sauerkraut and then a layer of the ribs and a final layer of potatoes.

Place the pan in the oven at 300 degrees for one and one-half hours.

Remove from oven, sprinkle with a high quality Hungarian paprika and serve hot.

It's another one-pot dish that makes a great fall or winter meal. A solid dark beer goes great with this entrée. I like Guinness Stout, a Porter or a Black or Brown Ale like St. Peter's Summer Ale.

GRANDMA PALMA'S RIZOT (RISOTTO) *Serves 8*

I always remember this meal served for a celebration such as a birthday, Easter, a baptism or holiday. My grandmother, at her house on 15th Street raised chickens, mostly Rhode Island Reds. They were a friendly and good natured breed. When I was young I would often visit the coop and play with the little chicks. They were raised for their meat and eggs. The eggs are brown and they were always in great supply. The hens weighed about 6 pounds and the roosters 8 to 9 pounds.

The day before grandma would be cooking her rizot she would butcher one of the old stewing hens. She knew the art well, because in her home country her family operated a butcher shop and she had worked in it from the time she was a young girl. I remember going to the store with her where she would quiz the butcher unrelentingly about freshness and the origination of the product she was purchasing. Then she would give it the 'old nose' test to determine the freshness. In those days there were real butchers behind the counter rushing around in the fresh, clean sawdust on the floor. I never quite understood the sawdust.

INGREDIENTS:

3 to 4 pound stewing hen, meat cut into bite size pieces

4 tablespoons of Olive oil

1 large onion, finely chopped

3 stalks of celery, chopped

6 cloves of garlic, finely chopped

Zest of one orange, minced

Juice of one orange

16 oz. can of tomato sauce

1 tablespoon tomato paste

Salt & pepper to taste

2 cups of Arborio rice

2 quarts warmed chicken broth

6—8 oz. parmesan cheese

Place the olive oil in a frying pan on medium, add the chicken and brown slowly. Separately brown the onion, celery, orange zest and garlic. Add the chicken to this combination along with the tomato sauce, tomato paste, orange juice and one cup of the broth into a large pan. Add the salt & pepper to taste.

Simmer for one-hour. Then add the rice and continue to simmer, adding more of the chicken broth as the rice consumes the liquid. This is a key time in the preparation. Make certain that you have added a sufficient amount of broth or the rice will burn. If you exhaust the broth simply use a little boiling water. This is not exactly like the risotto that is so common in fine Italian restaurants, as this recipe is more on the soupy side. When the rice is done, like pasta, it should be al dente. Proceed to add½ the parmiggiano and½ the parsley and mix gently. Then put a lid on the pan and let it set for 10 to 15 minutes. This will allow the flavors to combine and to rest. Serve in warmed soup bowls immediately, adding the remaining parmiggiano and parsley over each individual bowl.

I suggest serving the rizot with a tossed salad and hot garlic bread. Zinfandel is the perfect wine to compliment this dish and it was recently discovered that the Zinfandel grape has its roots in Croatia. Just a few years ago DNA testing proved that Zinfandel, America's Heritage grape," actually originated in Croatia where the name of the grape is crljenak kastelanski and the wine is called Oatia.

Octopus has long been a delicacy of the Croatian people.

To really know and enjoy octopus you need to catch one yourself and there is nowhere better than Puget Sound to do so. I learned from Tony Pule Barcott, who held himself out as a professional octopus hunter. We would pursue these creatures at low tide when you could reach the caves where they lived. And you always knew where they dwelled by the pile of clam shells at the entrance. Tony would bring a long pole about 16' in length. He would then tie a colorful bandana to one end that was filled with bluestone (sodium chloride). When the chemical mixed with water or moisture it would give off an officious order that made the octopus angry and it would madly rush out of the cave just as we would throw a heavy net over it. Sometimes it was so big that the net wasn't large enough to capture it and it would run off. The ones that we did catch became furious and tried desperately to escape. However, once we had the net over it we never lost one.

Once when I was about ten years old we were fishing on West Beach which is fairly shallow and we were dragging the bottom. We caught a myriad of strange looking fish including an octopus. It weighed about 40 pounds. Octopi's legs have rows of suckers on them and as I was investigating the strange looking beast it reached out and attached firmly to my boot. My only escape was to pull my leg out of the boot. My grandfather retrieved the boot and I learned an interesting lesson about putting things where they don't belong.

INGREDIENTS:

Two legs of an octopus

2 tbls. Olive oil

1 medium sized yellow onion, chopped

6 garlic cloves, chopped

2 tablespoons of chopped parsley

1 cup white rice

2 cups fish broth

Pound the octopus with a butcher maul or similar hammer to make tender like you would a round steak. This will take about 15 to 20 minutes.

Cut up the legs in bite size pieces

In a frying pan add the olive oil and on medium heat brown the onion, parsley and garlic. When the onion is translucent add the octopus. Add broth as needed. In 30 minutes (before the octopus is done) add the rice. If there is not sufficient juice then add fish broth as required and cook until done about 30 minutes.

OCTOPUS SALAD

This is another of my favorites. It is tasty and nutritious. We often fixed this on the F/V Cypress whenever we captured one of these peculiar creatures.

INGREDIENTS:

2 octopus legs

1 medium purple onion, sliced

½ cup of sliced green onions, chopped

4 garlic cloves, diced

½ cup olive oil

2 tablespoons of wine vinegar

Salt & heavy grind of pepper

Take legs of the octopus and pound as described above. Place the pounded meat into salted boiling water that barely covers it. Cook for about one hour or until tender. Place in refrigerator for a few hours until cooled. Cut into ¼ inch slices; add purple onion, green onion, and garlic. Season with olive oil and vinegar. Salt and pepper to taste. Refrigerate for six hours or so. We generally serve this as an appetizer. My mother loved this preparation and I would often prepare it for her.

This green vegetable dish was almost always served when fish was the main entrée. My grandmother grew all of the ingredients in her backyard garden. Today I can buy most of the items all year long in order to serve the dish whenever I choose.

INGREDIENTS:

5 tablespoons of olive oil

6-8 Kale leaves, beet greens, or Swiss chard or combination thereof.

1 pound Fava beans

1 pound String beans

2 cups Peas

4 medium sized Red potatoes, quartered

1 onion, chopped

4 garlic cloves, chopped

Salt & pepper

In a large pot of boiling salted water add the Red potatoes and cook about 20 minutes, add the greens, string beans and fava beans and cook until tender. Place in colander, drain completely. Place in covered bowl and keep warm.

Separately sauté the onion and garlic cloves in a tablespoon of olive oil. When the onion is translucent add either fresh or frozen peas and cook until the peas are tender but still firm, eight to ten minutes.

Add the peas and onion mixture to the other vegetables and toss gently with salt & pepper and 3–4 tablespoons of olive oil.

In the northwest and Alaska the Dungeness crab is a favorite of seafood connoisseurs. It is plentiful and delicious by all standards. When I fished in Southeastern Alaska we were always able to catch a few crabs for the galley table. And when we did catch a mess of crabs the cook often prepared this savory dish.

The Dungeness crab averages about 2½ pounds except around Kachemak Bay in Central Alaska near Homer where they would often average nearly 4 pounds. These little crustaceans are found from the Aleutian Islands to Central and Southeastern Alaska, in British Columbia, and the states of Washington, Oregon and northern California.

INGREDIENTS:

1 lb. of shelled Dungeness crab.

2 quarts of chicken broth

2 cups of Arborio rice

1 medium onion, finely chopped

1 cup dry white wine

1 cup parmesan cheese, shredded

6 garlic cloves

2 tablespoons of butter

3 tablespoons of parsley, minced

Salt and Pepper

1 cup green peas, fresh or frozen

olive oil for sauteéing

Heat the broth in a medium sized sauce pan.

In a large heavy pot over medium heat, sauté the chopped onions, garlic and butter for 3 minutes or until the onion is translucent.

Add the rice and stir frequently about two minutes and then immediately add the wine and stir until the wine has evaporated. Continue stirring the warm broth into the rice as it is consumed. This takes about 40 minutes of continual stirring. Some cooks pour all the broth in at one time or use a pressure cooker. That works but it doesn't give the risotto the same richness and buttery taste as when you slowly stir as described here.

When the rice is just about done carefully stir in the green peas and after about 10 minutes add the Dungeness crab and the ½ the minced parsley leaves. Salt and pepper to taste.

Finally add ½ the parmesan cheese and cover for ten minutes.

Ladle into pre-heated bowls, add a little more cheese and parsley on the top and serve immediately.

This dish can easily be the main entrée or in smaller portions it can be a side dish with grilled or barbequed salmon, baked halibut or a meat dish such as short ribs.

As for a wine either a light red, such as a pinot or merlot or a green Chardonnay goes wonderfully. I prefer the Francis Ford Coppola Rosso Classic, a delicious old school California red. In the summer I will often choose a good quality French Rosé.

UNCLE TONY'S TURKEY DRESSING

I have cooked at least 50 Thanksgiving and holiday turkeys and have used this recipe every single time. Actually I really don't need a recipe any longer and sometimes I will even vary the recipe, but not much. It is savory and compliments the basic holiday dishes that accompany the turkey. My Uncle Tony was a perfectionist and each item had to be perfectly sliced and diced.

After he retired as the skipper of the Veribus he became the cook for Delmar Cole on the fishing vessel Radio. He loved to cook and prided himself on the delicious meals that he prepared.

INGREDIENTS TO DRESS A 20 TO 25 POUND TURKEY:

1½ loaves of stale white French (I take it out of the package 2 days before I need it and place each slice on a counter or out of the way until it is hard almost like toast)

Cut or break each slice of bread into 5 or 6 pieces.

Two pounds of mild link sausage

½ pound of dried apricots or cherries—chopped

2 quarts of chicken broth

1 Large yellow onion—finely diced

4 garlic cloves—finely diced

3 carrots—finely diced

2 cups celery—diced

1 tablespoon dried sage

1 bunch parsley—chopped roughly

Salt & pepper

In a large pan bring two quarts of water to a boil. Place the sausages in the water for 5 minutes. Remove and rinse the fat from them and cut into bite sized pieces.

In a large frying pan sauté the onions, garlic, carrots, celery and dried fruit in a little olive oil. About 20 minutes on medium low heat. Set aside.

In the same pan brown the sausage for 12- 15 minutes.

Combine the above in a very large bowl or pan and add the bread mixing it in thoroughly and adding the chicken broth a little at a time along with the sage and parsley. Salt and pepper to taste. Refrigerate overnight and it will be ready to stuff into the turkey the next morning.

ELLIE'S KING CRAB ENCHILADAS *Serves 12*

Ellie was the wife of our assistant superintendent in Seldovia. On Sunday evening she would often fix dinner for the management team and occasionally I would be there to enjoy these great seafood feasts. My favorite dish was her King Crab Enchiladas. She used merus legs which I explained earlier are the 'prime cut' of the King crab.

INGREDIENTS:

12 burrito size flour tortillas

24 King Crab merus legs (shelled)

12 oz. shredded jack or pepper jack cheese

1—20 oz. can of green enchilada sauce

1—16 oz. container sour cream

1 bunch of green onions, chopped

Preheat oven to 350 degrees

Lay tortillas on a flat surface

Place 2 of the crab legs in each of the tortillas along with the cheese (be sure to hold back some cheese to sprinkle on top of the tortillas)

Roll the tortillas so that the crab legs are held securely inside the tortillas

Place the rolled tortillas side by side in a 9 x 13 inch baking pan

Pour the green enchilada sauce over all the tortillas (it should cover completely)

Bake covered at 350 degrees for 30 minutes

Uncover the enchiladas and cook for an additional 15 minutes

Serve hot, garnish with the sour cream and chopped green onions

BUSTER'S BREAD PUDDING   *Serves 6-8*

Buster Swan was a 350 pound giant of a man who year round wore bib overalls and a white T-shirt. His cooking skills were honed in the hot galleys of salmon fishing boats.

Buster cooked for Grandpa Tasovac on the Veribus when I was ten years old. I would scrub his pots and pans and mop the galley decks. He would often give me tastes of his dishes in process.

I am not 100% certain of the food measurements, as he was never very exacting in that department. However, whatever he prepared always seemed to turnout marvelously. Dessert or anything that resembled it was a treat and not often served aboard the boats. Buster always tried to make the meals special. He realized how hard the crew worked and how they appreciated their meals. My grandfather had a saying, "You never make a season by scrimping on the grub bill".

Preheat the oven to 350 degrees. The enormous galley stove roared at full blast 7 x 24, so Buster didn't ever have to preheat the oven. This mighty stove warmed the whole cabin and sometimes it got terribly hot in the galley especially after having washed up all the dishes and pots and pans.

It was a long time ago when I worked in Buster's galley and my memory of this recipe is unclear. Yet, I have successfully used this recipe many times over the years.

INGREDIENTS:

A loaf of day old bread (Remove the crusts) Butter the bread on both sides.

3 cups milk

4 eggs + 3 egg yolks

⅔ cup sugar

About½ cup of Irish whiskey

1½ teaspoons vanilla extract

2 teaspoon cinnamon

2 cups of raisins.

In a large bowl whisk together the milk, whole eggs, egg yolks, whiskey, sugar and vanilla.

Place a layer of the bread in a large pan and continue to layer it up to about one inch from the top. Pour the milk mixture over the bread slowly letting the bread absorb the mixture.

Place the pan in the middle of a large roasting pan and pour boiling water in the roasting pan until it is about half way up the sides of the pan. Bake until the mixture is set about 45 minutes to an hour depending on the oven. It took a little longer in the old oil ranges.

To serve you can prepare an elegant sauce that you can easily find in a fancy cook book or you can find a can of condensed milk, if they still make it, and pour a little over the top of a hearty slice.

APPLE CAKE

Finally, I want to share my Grandmother's scrumptious apple cake. I remember vividly visiting her after school on 15th Street and eating her apple cake. My mother also prepared it frequently in the fall of the year from fresh apples.

INGREDIENTS:

4 cups diced apples

2 eggs

1 cup shortening

2 cups sugar

2 cups flour, sifted

1 tablespoons cinnamon

½ cup walnuts

1 cup raisins

2 teaspoons soda

1 teaspoon vanilla

½ teaspoons salt

½ teaspoon nutmeg

Cream together the shortening, sugar, vanilla and eggs.

Sift the flour, cinnamon, nutmeg and salt and add to the creamed mixture.

Mix with 2 teaspoon of hot water and the soda.

Add the apples and raisins and then pour the mixture into a 9" x 13" pan which has been greased and floured. Sprinkle the top with the walnuts and bake at a temperature of 350 degrees for 45 minutes.

FIRST TRIP SKIPPER -- Gary Keister, 22, takes last look ashore before leaving dock at
Farwest Cannery on his first trip north as a captain. Gary is believed the youngest skipper
in the Anacortes fleet this year. The crew of the "Whitworth" is composed mainly of basketball players, plus one football player and one wrestler for balance. Members of the
crew are; Ron Behrbaum, 6'4"; Joe Blum, 6'3"; "Hod" Pearson, 6'; Bob Pearson, 6'7";
Gary Keister, Captain, 6'5" and Jack Kidder the only crew member who drinks coffee, so
his vital statistics are unrecorded.

Captain Keister said, "We may not be the best fishermen in the fleet, but we think we're
the biggest."

Anacortes American **news clipping describing first voyage**

Departing Anacortes

Grand Back Then

It was grand back then
those post-war forties.
Life was secure
in that closely knit
island fishing village.

Still today
it's comforting to return,
traveling through the rich soiled
Skagit Valley, crossing the
Swinomish Slough
and driving down the singular
avenue called Commercial
where the air is fresh,
and the sea-salt smell consuming.
Oh those familiar smells of childhood,
long gone,
save my well of memories.

As I wander an abandoned
weather beaten cannery,
its wet-red paint faded a dull blush
from decades of battering
by harsh salt and wind driven seas.
I can see the fresh Sockeye
unloading at the cannery dock,
tons of icy sea-water bathing

their sleek blue-back bodies.
Conveyed to worn wooden bins,
tall and tawny young men
in tattered, yellow, rain gear
shovel crystal clear ice
on the precious cargo.

In the dimly lit fish house
the stank of blood and guts,
as the glorious Reds
are butchered and sliced
while old bent women in black
and blue kerchiefs hand pack the
blood-red meat.
The clinking tins move noisily
towards the clik-clik-clik
of the steel-grey seamer
and stacked onto rusting
metal pallets and shoved
in the asbestos coated,
tomb like chambers.
The cookers discharge
a scalding sizzling steam
on the piled high tins,
cooking the hearty flesh
yet preserving its dazzling
crimson color.